D1648589

BOIL
THE FROG

DENNIS MCVICKER

Copyright © 2022 Dennis McVicker
All rights reserved
First Edition

PAGE PUBLISHING
Conneaut Lake, PA

First originally published by Page Publishing 2022

ISBN 978-1-6624-7889-5 (pbk)
ISBN 978-1-6624-7890-1 (digital)

Printed in the United States of America

DO NOT GO GENTLE INTO THAT GOOD NIGHT

Dylan Thomas

Do not go gentle into that good night,
Old age should burn and rave at close of day.
Rage, rage against the dying of the light.

Though wise men at their end know dark is right,
Because their words had forked no lightning they
Do not go gentle into that good night.

Good men, the last wave by, crying how bright
Their frail deeds might have danced in a green bay,
Rage, rage against the dying of the light.

Wild men who caught and sang the sun in flight,
And learn, too late, they grieved it on its way,
Do not go gentle into that good night.

Grave men, near death, who see with blinding sight
Blind eyes could blaze like meteors and be gay,
Rage, rage against the dying of the light.

And you, my father, there on the sad height,
Curse, bless, me now with your fierce tears, I pray.
Do not go gentle into that good night.
Rage, rage against the dying of the light.

WELCOME

Are you ready to save your own life? Are you ready to quit the very things that are ruining your life? Are you ready to see an "impossible" situation and understand that it's not only possible, it's likely that you can complete it?

If you answered yes to any or all those questions, congratulations on taking the first steps to a new you! Sound impossible? I can guarantee you that it's not. It just seems overwhelming, but don't worry, I'll show you how to be able to look at situations that look like it is impossible (and I'll show you how to take this word out of your vocabulary) and be able to take it one little step at a time.

Before going any further (read the whole paragraph before putting this book back down), let me say a couple of things, I am a US Navy Veteran. As such, I "cuss like a sailor." I use "foul language," "bad words," or "cuss." In person, I swear a lot; however, I did not drop one "F-bomb" in this book, and I'm proud of that, but I do throw in the occasional "cuss" word for emphasis. I use them as they should be, as expressive words. Some words you just can't substitute. I did keep it at a minimal because I know some people are offended by them, so I promise it's only used when necessary.

Also, the other thing I want is to encourage those of you on the fence that have had failures in the past. These kinds of setbacks can create skepticism that new things can work for them, But the past is where that is, and that's exactly where it belongs. Right back there in the past, a memory; dust in the wind (Thanks, Kansas!).

You are making a conscious decision *right now* to change your life, perhaps even save your life. So put a wall up, in your mind, and put that wall directly touching your back, right behind you. There is no backward now. Now, you can only move forward toward those doors of possibility. If you are not there yet, don't worry; you will be.

Your mind is the engine to everything, and it functions in the exact manner you have it set for. It's up to you to get into your own head and reset the controls back to default at first, then into super mode. Once you harness its power and take control, you will understand that you have had this power your whole life yet you have chosen not to use it—yet. Those days are over.

Once you open yourself to the idea that you can succeed in anything you do, the infinite becomes possible. What you used to find "impossible" was really just feeling overwhelmed at a vast problem you were staring at with no idea even how to start. Very simply, you start where you start and just do the rest until that seemingly impossible task gets chipped away, and then all of a sudden, it's completed.

You'll understand that now is what matters, and actions—not words—are what matter. The procrastinators have stolen this phrase and reversed it, but it's time for you to say the correct way:

Don't put off until tomorrow what you can do today.
(Benjamin Franklin)

The first thing to understand is that this is not a program that has universal steps that apply to everyone. Everyone's situation is different, and every program will be different. Mostly because it's not actually a "program" in the sense of the word; they are daily goals you set for yourself. Put them all together and it appears to be many steps, but it's just goals. Goals that are completely achievable because you set them yourself, based on your own performance.

Very simply stated, this will work for you because you only have to be better than the person you were yesterday. Some people will have to start extremely slow; some will be able to go big right away. *Your current situation will not stop you from doing this! I don't care if you are one of those people that have to use an electric cart to get around the grocery store. You can do this too!*

Today's effort is tomorrow's body. If you want to be lazy today, that's the body you will have tomorrow. Everything you do is based on your effort. *You* put in the work, and *you* get the results. Nobody is doing this for you, and that is something that you should be very proud of. Break the habits of "I can't" and change that to "I can," or at the very least, "I'll try until I can." Allow the idea that you can become fertile in your mind, and it will grow exponentially.

I want this is in bold, so you all see this. I want you to find a way to see this phrase *daily*. Print it out, embroider it on a pillow, take a picture and make it your screensaver, or make it your phone lock/home screen. I don't care how you do it, just read this every day:

> The only person you are competing with is the person you were yesterday.

So now that you know you have no excuses, there is no reason not to save your own life, right? So are you going to read this and act or are you going to read this and get discouraged? Either way, understand this. Not one thing on this Earth, or other planets for that matter, is stopping you from being healthy but yourself. That's the first thing you need to get right mentally. You are in this situation and purchased/borrowed this book because your life decisions have made you afraid for your own life enough to act, and I salute you for it, because that is a terrific motivator.

Moreover, you don't have to do this alone! There are social media support groups that are set up (just for people reading this book!) where we can all show our successes and give support to each other so you can make it happen.

There are walkers and there are talkers. Action-takers and storytellers. What kind of person do you want to be? I choose to walk, literally and figuratively. Thanks so much for joining the many of us that have chosen to take control of their life and congratulations!

QUICK NOTE ABOUT THIS BOOK

Honestly, until it was written, I thought this book was just going to be about my weight loss journey. However, once I started writing it down and showing it to people for their feedback, I think we were all surprised that it dove much deeper than that.

I will definitely go through the steps I took to get the weight off, but you have to understand, just as I realized when I wrote it out, that it's about your entire life as a whole. The weight loss is just an effect of *Boil the Frog*.

The navigation of this book (on a timeline basis) will go back and forth, skipping around my journey in a non-sequential order. I was struggling with what to do about this until I realized that's okay. This book will go in order a little bit and then reflect on other things. I can't blame it; my mind is working just like I asked it to, which will make sense to you later.

Bottom line, I wanted to let you know, that yes, I know this book skips around a little bit here and there on my journey; however, the tangents I make and the roads I lead you through are extremely relevant.

I didn't want to just say, "This is what I did." That's pretty uninteresting, and frankly, it's evolved into being much deeper than that. So please enjoy the twists, turns, flashbacks, flash forwards, creative thinking exercises, critical thinking exercises, comfort zone exercises, my tough love trying to motivate you, me calling you out on your excuses, me calling you fat, me calling you lazy, etc. you get as you go through this book.

Of course, you can also always just do what I do and read the whole book to make up your own mind about how you want to use the information before acting. I tried not to add filler, though I do repeat important concepts so you can understand how important those points are. I wanted the core concepts to be simple and easy to understand and implement. I didn't want this to be long-winded for the sake of making a longer book. This book will be exactly how long it needs to be to get you the ideas and concepts you can use right now to change your life little by little each day until six months from now, people will not recognize you from top to bottom. Well, probably your face, but that's it.

So while I tried to take you straight through my journey, it didn't end up that way. You'll learn that obstacles and problems are just road bumps to be felt, passed, and forgotten. With that all being said, please enjoy your journey through my journey.

THE FABLED BOILED FROG

I have not been able to find this actual experiment (allegedly conducted in the nineteenth century), where it was done, or if it was even done or something somebody made up and sounded good. However, the premise is true if you know how to apply it to everyday life.

The fabled boiled frog experiment is as follows (and don't really do this for real. This is a metaphorical expression as far as everyone is concerned. *Do not actually boil frogs!* Not even gonna say please—just don't): the premise is that if you place a frog into a boiling pot of water, the frog will instantly jump out, and most likely be burned in the process. If you put a frog into room temperature water and slowly increase the heat, the frog will stay in the water until it is boiled to death.

Pretty morbid idea to begin with; someone must have been really bored in the science lab. I can just imagine walking in there and saying, "So...what's the end game here fellas?" But again, I haven't been able to find this actual experiment, nor would I want to—what a horrible idea (but interesting concept nonetheless). Most likely, it's is another one of those pop culture phenomena that turn falsehoods into truth just from their popularity, also known as the Mandela effect.

The Mandela effect occurs when a person believes that their distorted memories are, in fact, accurate recollections. They can clearly remember events that happened differently or events that never occurred at all. The bottom line is that the Mandela effect does not involve lying or deception, just misremembering.

In actuality, the frog couldn't actually jump out of a pot of boiling water because of the protein in its skinny legs would solidify and it would be stuck, so I fully understand that this is not a real thing, but the idea and notion, when changed into an ideology, is unbelievably effective. Regardless of how the fabled frog tale came to pass, its premise, when properly applied to your life as a whole, is relevant to everything. Including diet and exercise—especially these because they are the very things people quit the most.

Now, I know, based on mathematics and science and the laws of probability, that at least half of you reading this have tried something else and it didn't work for you. It's just a universal certainty that I'm willing to lose face on if it's incorrect. Here's why.

When people decided to do something which they have been putting off, they are trying to boil the frog by just throwing it in the pot. They go all in. "I'm going to cut out this from my diet," "I'm going to exercise daily," "I'm going to this, going to that"—it's always the same, usually.

If you succeeded going this route, congratulations! This is only going to help you more. However, if you did not, here is the premise you need to understand before you even get started.

Mental preparation is the beginning of this, and not fast-boiling the frog is the biggest part of this. *The number one reason that diets and exercise regimens fail is that people strain themselves because they went too fast at the beginning, and when they don't see the results they want right away, they just quit.*

How do you overcome this? That's right: You don't flash boil the frog; you give yourself the best chance to succeed, and besides, you feel great after. After the initial shock to the system (which usually lasts about one to two weeks), you start to feel better little by little each day. A week goes by, maybe two, and you decide to turn up the heat a little bit.

That is the secret to success. You can't eat a whole elephant in one sitting, you must eat it one bite at a time. It took years to get where you are now, it will take a while to get out of it. The healthy way.

CRAWLING

Why not walking? Of course, you crawl first before you can walk. Just like life, you have to start out slow. In fact, slowness, building, and leveling up is the entire basis of *Boil the Frog*. This section will be critical for some people. This is the proverbial train wheel's initial spin, trying to gain traction representing motion about to occur. *Chugga*

This is more of a mental action than a physical one. It is the very moment you decide to act and actually do it. What will your action be? It has to be something you wouldn't normally do, that's relatively easy to do, and that you inform others about. Make yourself accountable! A shared goal/action/habit is ten times more likely to be successful than the ones you keep secret. Once you commit to it and commit to it publicly, your reputation is at stake. You now have skin in the game, literally and figuratively.

Update your friends and family about it. Share your goals on social media! There is always a group of people trying to do this exact same thing. Find a hashtag you like that's relatable and go with it. My favorite is *#mindset*. Though for my own selfishness's sake, I hope you use the *#boilthefrog* so I can see all my fine people's progress. I can't think of a more fulfilling way than to see you all succeeding together.

The best way is to find like-minded individuals that will do it with you. You are each other's crutch. They will motivate you, and you will motivate them. If you don't have that person physically nearby, you can have that person online or through chat or through email. Just be able to communicate daily, and your chances of success will drastically increase.

Compare challenges and share ideas of things you can do to expand your knowledge to each other. When properly taken, this journey will allow you to create very effective habits and techniques that will do well for anyone. Expanding comfort zones are the most fun. See how far you can push each other's zone out there. Come up with funny things to do with each other like random action texts that the other person has to do, like "dance on the table for twenty seconds." Your imagination is your limit.

I went solo on my journey, so it's possible; it's just more difficult, and no one texted me to dance on a table or "Shatner!" Do not be dissuaded if you don't have a partner. Some people work better alone, and I completely understand. If you can do that and stay on the ball like I can, no problem; go that route. I have proven that you can if you want to, but then I've always been a loner.

However, whether you are alone or with a partner, posting about it, telling people about it is the best way to keep yourself accountable and keep you motivated. This is something people will actually support you in doing, unlike "starting a business," which everyone seems to just skip that post, but I digress. *Ahem*

Post it on your social media or write it on a whiteboard if online is not your thing: #Day1 "whatever your goal is." Your goal is your goal, and you need to find out what that is before you start. My goal when I started was literally quite simple. I love my 36W x 32L cargo jeans from Wrangler, and I couldn't find them anywhere. They just stopped selling them in the stores I went to. Apparently, I was their only customer in that area, and I wasn't buying enough to keep the demand. I do have an odd size pants; though I usually settle for what's available (32w x 33L currently *wink*), I also had become so overweight that I could not sit down without unbuttoning and unzipping them.

So I had to find a different pair of pants. I found some cargo pants (not jeans) and bought the next size up, size 38 waist. I brought them home, anxiously optimistic that I didn't have to suck in my gut to put on my pants anymore and slipped them on.

"You have got to be kidding me," I exclaimed. They were tight. I had waited so long to buy new pants that I skipped that size and needed the size above them.

My mission went from finding new cargo jeans, to fitting into *these* cargo jeans. That was roughly in February, and I told no one about it because it's embarrassing. It is embarrassing to admit to everyone that you have a weight problem, but you are going to do something about it with no idea whether you will succeed or not. I completely get it because I kept it to myself and didn't do anything about it for months! I didn't actually start doing something about it until May. That's when I told my wife about it, and put myself on the hook, and guess what? That's when I started actually making progress.

It doesn't have to be on social media—some people just refuse to participate (lookin' at you, Jeremy)—just let someone else know your goal. The more you care about them, the better. Tell them your plan and tell them to keep you accountable. Anything you can do to put that energy out into the universe. Some people scoff when I say that phrase (I used to be one of them), but I have firsthand experience with this, that it really works.

Keep track and keep updating either in person or on social media. Take pictures, take videos, just post something about it, or share it with someone else. Trust me, it is far easier to carry your goal if you have people helping you, even if it's just moral support. If you are a procrastinator by nature and usually put things off, this will help you daily to remind yourself that you are making yourself better each day.

So what was the crawling for me? For me, it was two things, both just as important as the other. First was the day I decided to walk to the store for the first time. I found myself embarrassed to tell my wife I was doing it for some reason, and she looked pretty confused herself about it. But that's how it starts, and like I said, I understand that it *is* embarrassing to finally admit to another person that you desperately need to change your life for the better or it's going to be over far shorter than it needs to be. The more embarrassed you are to say it, the more you *need* to say it. The second I will tell you after you read the Emmitt Smith/Michael Jordan story in this section.

This is all you need to start your crawl: Just do one thing a day you wouldn't normally do. Anyone reading this is either reading it again or reading it for the first time because you *know* you need to work on yourself. For some of you, it may be absolutely medically necessary to work on yourself daily. That's really all it takes; start crawling your way back.

Some people have trouble just walking right away so this is what I want you to do. **It doesn't matter how many steps you take in the beginning, as long as those steps and actions are more than you did the day before.** *This is in bold because this a very critical point.* It may take some of you months to be able to even start setting daily steps goals, but this is how you get there.

When I say steps, I don't mean just walking either. Steps as in actions you take. Some reading this book may not even be able to walk, either by weight or by physical limitations. It doesn't matter. You can still achieve your goals as long as you are willing to take action. Moving slowly is still moving forward, and that's all that matters. You can *always* slow down, just don't stop.

Dan Lok says many things in his books, but one in particular stood out to me: *"If you set a goal and you have a clear path on how to achieve that goal, your goal is not big enough."* Read that again and memorize it and motivate yourself. For instance, if you have to use an electronic cart to get around the store, that should be your first goal to get well enough to walk around to do your shopping. If you don't believe that is possible, that is why you can't do it! You can literally do anything you set your mind to. Once you turn that phrase around, you begin to believe it's possible.

If you accomplishing your goal makes you drop to your knees and cry, that goal was big enough. That sense of achievement cannot be duplicated in any other action you can take on this planet or any other for that matter. Setting and accomplishing what you thought was impossible just a few months ago is the most amazing feeling you will ever feel.

Just like effort, you will know if you gave enough. I sometimes find myself laying on my exercise mat doing my post-workout stretching/yoga and just have to lay there in a pool of sweat, breathing hard. I don't have to guess if I put enough effort in on a daily basis, and neither do you. You know when you gave enough; don't cheat yourself.

That is exactly what the "crawl" is. It's giving your mind and body a jolt, letting it know that change is coming. This is a crucial step toward your success. I don't even want you to read past this section until you have mentally committed, until you have made your crawl. You have to make some effort to stop the momentum of your life moving in a wrong direction and start to crawling back to your life. You may feel weak and not up to the task when you start, but I guarantee you that if you fully commit to *Boil the Frog*, you will look back at the person you are right now in six months and be disgusted. Just thinking of the years of life you wasted being who you were and thinking of all of the things you could have achieved. Then you will sigh and then you'll dismiss that and move on.

That is the result of *Boil the Frog*. Your mental focus and abilities will continuously increase to the point where your mind becomes fertile to new ideas. You break down the walls you have been programmed to build for yourself and strip away the layers of defense you have built up over the years like a force field against the cruel world.

Get inside your own head and hit the reset button and then take the controls and set them to whatever you want to be. This is all possible. I have done this, and you can too. If you don't believe it's possible, you're right, and if you do believe it's possible, you're also right.

Free your mind. Mindset = a fertile mind open for seeds of knowledge to grow.

> *Open your mind to me, Quaid.*
> —Kwato, Mars Resistance Rebel
> Leader, *Total Recall*

Back in the '90s Emmitt Smith reached out to Michael Jordan to learn about business from him. Mike said no problem and set a meeting place.

After they met, Emmitt asked, "How come we don't have meetings like this more often to learn and do business together?"

Mike answered, "What did you have to do to get this meeting?"

Emmitt said, "I had to call you to ask you for the information."
Mike said, "Exactly. If you had not done that we would not be
sitting down talking about business. You were humble enough to ask,
meaning you were willing to learn. I cannot teach someone who is not
willing to learn. You have to have a fertile mind before seeds can be
planted or you will never learn."
As the saying goes, "When the student is ready the teacher will appear."

Mindset = Fertile Mind. Mindset = Willingness to learn. Mindset = Ready for the next challenge. Mindset = Knowing you will succeed. *#mindset.*

Now that you know that story, the second crawl I did was read a book called *Mindset: The New Psychology of Success* by Carol S. Dweck. Interesting thing about me is that I am probably the slowest learner I know, which may surprise people that know me because I think quick and act even quicker. However, when I first read that book, it didn't really sink in. I was skeptical about it, but I was going to give it a try. Ironically, I needed to read that book to be in the right mindset to absorb what the book was trying to tell me. So read it twice if you have to, but read it. Because even though I was skeptical, it did plant the seed in my mind. My mind was just fertile enough for the seed to take hold.

Slowly, over time, that seed started to develop, and one day, I was just in the mindset. Don't know when it happened, but just *click*, I'm there. The only difference between that working and that not working even though I was skeptical about it was allowing the idea that this could possibly work. Just a crack in the door, just a sliver of light; just from the notion "I will try." I *let* it sink in. I had just enough of a small patch of fertile mind that it took hold. Just the little ideas that I was willing to change and just enough belief that I could.

I was the exact same as many of you, always trying but not succeeding, and I couldn't figure out why. I just wasn't ready yet, and maybe that is you right now. But if you put this book down because you think you are not ready, do what you need to do to pick it back up. That is your first crawl. Get yourself in the mental state necessary to be receptive to change and learning.

For most reading this, so far in life, you have been moving backward, that is why the initial *chugga* crawl action is so important. You are stopping your negative progress and turning things around. You are stopping momentum and pushing it the other way. It will not be easy to stop that motion and push it the other way, but it is not impossible. In fact, that word means nothing to me now. Everything is possible because I believe it is.

Just like in the movie *The Matrix,* the main character, Neo, was believed to be what the other characters in the movie called "the One"—a person who was capable of incredible things, all of which Neo (anagram of One, by the way) did not believe. They kept telling him he had this great power, like I'm telling you now, and he didn't believe it. Over and over, he kept shaking his head in disbelief.

In the movie, Agents protect The Matrix and seek out and kill all hackers that infiltrate the system trying to free other souls. They are part of the system, so they are "invincible," they can't be beat, and they can't be killed. They jump into a person plugged into the Matrix. Even if you manage to kill them, they just jump somewhere else. They kept telling Neo he was The One, and he could not only face them, he could kill them. He still didn't believe it after the infamous "I know Kung Fu," line.

There came a point when he had to know it for himself. There came a point where he let the sliver of light through the door into his mind and decided to try. At that moment, you see the gears turning in his head, and halfway up the stairs to run away, he turned around to face the "invincible" Agent Smith. He did this even though he was told that every single man or woman who has ever faced and fought an agent, everyone who has stood their ground, has died. He knew that everyone before him had failed doing what he was about to try, and he turned around, anyway.

> TRINITY. What is he doing?
> MORPHEUS. He is beginning to believe.

Did he get his ass kicked? Hell yeah; it's an agent, people! But he didn't die, and he proved it was possible because he believed it was and he did it. I'm not asking you all to fight a fictional agent, I'm just asking you to believe in yourself to make small changes every day for an overall better you. Let that sliver of light through the door and try, you will be amazed with yourself.

> *You don't really know how much you can do, until you stand up and decide to really try."*
> —David Kovic (Kevin Kline) in the movie *Dave*

GET YOUR MIND RIGHT

In case I didn't hammer it home before, mindset is a huge part of this. In fact, it's the biggest part. You need to have a fertile mind to be able to accept new knowledge and a new way of thinking. You need to be ready to accept that you are going to change the very habits that are putting you in danger and are freely willing to do so. I cannot say this enough, *you have to be ready, and you have to believe in yourself,* or it will not work.

Have you ever tried to teach someone something that had zero interest in what you are trying to show them? The defiant stance, arms folded, blank look on their face, etc. The very posture of a loser is what I call that. You should always be willing to learn new things.

I have tried to show people that didn't want to learn, many times. Do you how many times I was teaching people that showed no interest and had a poor attitude in the beginning who were then actually surprised to find that they *were* interested and would like to know more? Exactly zero times. Not once.

The attitude you come with is what you will leave with. Your attitude will not improve unless you want it to. The phrase, "The world is what you make of it," is 100 percent accurate. You are *choosing* how to react to each obstacle you encounter throughout the day. Understand, it is on you. No outside force can affect your day unless you choose to let it do so. Anything can physically affect your body, but how your mind reacts is entirely on you.

If you have any doubt in your mind, don't even start. I'm not kidding. Part of this process is overhauling everything, and everything starts in the mind. Your attitude and view of the world is why you are where you are, right now. Every path on your own personal journey had forks in it, and you took whichever one you wanted. Now it's time to show your mind how to choose the right paths to take that lead to a mentally balanced, physically healthy body, and a life that is not only in order but in your complete control.

You can do whatever you need to accomplish this, but before you take one step, get your mind right. Your mind is a compass, and it has to be focused in the right direction if you want to get to where you want to be.

I already know what some of you are saying: "Get your mind right. Yeah, sure. Easy for you to say." Yes, it is easy to say, and it's damn hard to do. Nothing about changing your entire life is easy. Easy is what gave you a fat ass, easy is what gave you a shit entitlement attitude, and easy will not get you out of this rut and into your favorite pair of pants.

Getting your shit together is hard because life is hard when you let it. If you train to be easy than life *is* hard. If you train hard mentally and physically, life *is* easy because you are prepared for it. You are ready to fight the agents in your life that seem unbeatable. You are ready to tackle challenges other people shy away from because you are a train (**Chugga**), you are unstoppable, because you *know* you are unstoppable. (Suggested track: "Unstoppable" by Sia)

If you're ready now to start taking action, let's go! If you are not, get there first, and then let's start taking steps! Physical and mental! You just have to open the door just a crack. Let the idea that this will work for you enter the realm of possibility for you. and that little seed will grow and grow.

Start by writing down what you want to achieve. Make a goal list right now. The bigger the dream the better. Come up with something that you feel right now is "impossible" to do because it's so overwhelming. Like, run a marathon, lose two hundred pounds, get down to 10 percent body fat, date a "10"—you name it; the bigger the better. Come up with your "impossible" list, a literal list of everything you always wanted to achieve but had no idea how you could achieve it.

I have a goal of one day being the president of the United States, how can I achieve that when I'm not even in politics? No idea, that's because it's so big I don't understand how yet, but I do know it's one step at a time, and if I really set my mind to it, I can achieve it because I believe I can. Just like everything else, winners make their own "luck." Luck has nothing to do with achievement.

WALK THE WALK

There are walkers and there are talkers. Seldom people can be both, but they do exist. Point being, no one is going to take that first step for you. It's up to you. You do the work; you get the rewards. It literally is as simple as that.

How many of you have noticed that I say "you" a lot? There's a reason I am hammering this home: it is up to *you*. No one else is doing this for you. That should have been abundantly clear when you were getting your mind right. If you are not there yet, then stop. Getting your mind right is step 1, and you don't skip steps in this program.

Imagine your goals are a building, and you want that building to be solid. Each floor of that building is another goal to achieve. How can you construct any solid building without a proper foundation? You can't if you expect the building to last. Your mind is the foundation for your achievements. A horrible attitude makes a horrible foundation which makes a horrible building that will fall apart at the slightest problem.

Having the right attitude will form that solid foundation. Having that in place is key because we are now getting to the action phase. Here is where you turn your plans into actions. Up to this point, you have been part of the 80 percent that will never do anything. Now is the time you step into the 20 percent that take action. Now you become a leader, not a follower. Right now, you decide your own outcome. There is no "get to it later;" there is no "I'm just so busy right now." Like Arnold Schwarzenegger said in *Kindergarten Cop*: "There is no bathroom!"

As long as you understand that being in the correct mindset is part of walking the walk, you can get to the actual walking part of this process. It is just as simple as taking a step and going. You should have a solid idea of your own physical and mental capabilities and be able to phase into walking as you see fit. This is going to be as general as it can to apply to everyone.

There are many different tactics and styles to walking that you can use to keep yourself interested and keep your motivation up. For some people, you can find a safe route in your own neighborhood, just using a GPS and mapping out a route and distance. The amount of distance in the beginning does not matter. For that matter, the amount of distance in the end doesn't matter either. The only thing that matters is that it is an achievement for you, something better than you did before.

Before you actually get out there in the world and start walking you have to understand the world you are walking into. Like they say in boxing, *"protect yourself at* all *times."* Safety is your number 1 concern.

This is a world full of cars, we are just walking in it. You will eventually become hyperaware without even thinking about it, just like checking your blind spot to change lanes, but in the beginning, you need to train yourself to do so. Just like in driver's education (if that's still a thing).

First thing to be mindful of is to make sure you are walking in a safe neighborhood to begin with. I don't want you to sacrifice your safety because you happen to currently live in a high-crime area or an area with a lot of traffic and crossings you have to dodge. This is most important when you get to the running stage, and you will, trust me.

It's best to be able to walk your own neighborhood if it is safe to do so. If it is not, unfortunately, you will have the extra step of driving to a safer neighborhood. Hopefully, this doesn't apply to most of you, and you can just start right away.

Open up a GPS map of the safe area you chose or that you live in (you can use a phone or computer or a plain old paper map of the area) and look at all the routes in the area. Just make sure it is current and accurate. Most people live in a block configuration which makes things super easy. All streets are created by people so a definitive "lap" or route should be easy to find.

Whatever the shape of what you are looking at, find a lap. That is always the best way to start. If you are close to a school with a track, even better. Just know what the distance is. It's your choice. You know your fitness level; you know what you can and can't do. The initial goal of this step if you don't know your fitness level is to figure that out.

If you look at this action and think a lap or a walk around the block is way too far for you, then that's what you need to get started in the process. The only goal on everyone's agenda in the start is to find your starting point and log it.

Put it on the wall; put it on social media. Get the word out there that this is *#day1*. Today is the day I decided to turn my life around. Holding yourself publicly accountable is another motivation technique. The more people involved the better. Your true friends and family will cheer you on and support your effort. Some may even join you which is unbelievably helpful to keep up motivation. They don't even have to be with you; you can talk on the phone if you are not geographically in the same place.

If not, that's okay too. I went solo on my journey. You can, too, if you choose. But hold yourself accountable in some way where more than just you know your goals or the fact that you are trying to change your behaviors.

Now you know what you can do and where you will go. Now it's time to do it. Find a time each day you can do this, every day. You have to be consistent in your behaviors and good habits will start to form virtual grooves in your mind. Like a new record, you are setting new patterns in the wax of your fertile mind.

What your goal is today only has to be a little better than what your goal was yesterday. It's really that simple. If you are only able to walk to the refrigerator, get a drink (of water not soda), and come back and sit down because of your physical limitations, then your goal should be to walk there and walk back two times before sitting down again. Keep that goal until that becomes, not only a habit, but easier for you to do.

Once you accomplish your first goal and it becomes easy to achieve, then you step it up a little bit. It really doesn't matter what your goal is because you are continuously improving yourself on a daily basis. Those small corrections you are making are going to pay off big time down the road. Just like compound interest, little chunks over time create a really big chunk that most would have thought impossible.

Will it take a long time to get there this way? Absolutely, but nowhere near as long as it took you to get into the shape you are right now. It has taken you a lifetime of bad habits to get where you are now. If that wasn't true, you wouldn't have felt the need to get this book and put it into action. Maybe you were just curious when you picked it up or purchased it, but if you are this far, then you are already ready to act.

The quitter that was in you? You left it behind pages ago, and this is the new you. Just like once you get out on the road, that person that wanted to quit is sitting on a curb back there and the winner in you kept going. Ready to take on your goals, ready to save your own life, and ready to be the winner you were always meant to be. Congratulations so far, I'm proud of you, I believe in you, and I know you can do it. You would not be this far into this book if you couldn't do this. So embrace your new outlook on life and let's go!

EXAMPLE STARTING GOAL PLAN

I may have left a few people behind, so this section will walk through an example of someone starting from the absolute beginning. That way, it will show what I mean for those in better shape to follow and give a roadmap to those desperate to act but don't really know how to do it.

My favorite people to work with are people that need electric carts to do their grocery shopping or whatever shopping. They physically cannot walk the entirety of the store without the help of these carts. If this is you, your life is going to drastically change in the next few months, and I am so excited for you, you have no idea how true that is.

Some people have flat-out said, "I cannot exercise," or worse yet, from someone else saying, "They can't exercise." Anyone who is able to move any extremity is able to exercise. If you can walk to the fridge, you can exercise. If you are paralyzed, obviously you already have a physical therapy program you follow. Excluding that scenario, if you can physically stand up, you can exercise. Maybe that's all you can do, so that's your exercise.

So literal square 1 sample goal set here for people who can only physically stand up (if you can't stand up without help, then your goal is to be able to do so and then continue):

1. #Day1: Log the number of times you stood up in a day. Just place a notepad and pen/pencil next to where you sit and give a roman numeral slash mark for each time. Add

that up at the end of the day. Or use the notes section on your phone.

2. Day 2: Increase the number of times you stand up by 10 percent. If you stood up twenty times yesterday, standup and sit down two extra times with no other purpose than to add to your daily workload. You can do it all at once if you want, but get up and sit down with no reason to do so other than the fact you will get the exercise.

3. Day 3: Every day is better than the last so keep going. Add another 10 percent and always round up.

   You can't stand up .2 times, so always go up to the next number. So day 3 is 10 percent better than day 2 which was 10 percent better than day 1, so getting up twenty times on the first day equates to getting up twenty-five times on day 3. (20 x 10% = 2 + 20 = 22; 22 x 10% = 2.2 (round up always) = 3 + 22 = 25).

4. Day 4: 10 percent again. Twenty-eight stand ups this time.

5. Day 5: 10 percent again. Thirty-one stand ups this time.

Now I want you to notice something in this quick scenario. Even though you have only increased your effort 10 percent each day, in less than a week, you are standing up more than 50 percent more than you were when you started. You should also notice that it's getting a little bit easier at this point.

This will be a continual increase until this exercise has lost its practicality. You can't keep doing the same things and expect things to change. No one wants to spend all day standing up and sitting down. So you need to escalate things as soon as you are ready, in whatever shape you are in.

Like I said, this is just an example of how you can start from your current state and how to increase your exercising slowly so your body can handle it. I can't tell you how many people I know decide to get in the gym or out on the road and they go so hard so fast that they are miserable and just quit.

My friend Randy made this mistake, and he could barely walk downhill. He decided to start exercising again so he went to the gym near his house and signed up. When he did, they informed him that it comes with one free consultation with a "trainer." Whomever he was working with had no idea what they were doing. They made him do a full workout with another student even after explaining he was over sixty and hadn't exercised in years. Again, he could barely walk, rise, get out of bed without great pain. I told him that is exactly the wrong approach; you have to get in slowly. Your first few exercises or trips to the gym should be so light that it should almost feel like a waste of time.

Please listen to me, I have seen this mistake and even made this mistake myself. I know I am motivating the hell out of you, I know you are ready to go. I mean I'm talking about trains and being unstoppable so let's primal scream and get some!

Great, have the attitude, but with great power comes great responsibility. Your mind has become a race car and wants to rev your body to the max now that it's motivated. But you have to understand that you are starting in a residential section. You have to go through the neighborhood before you can get to the highway and really open things up. Drive carefully through here, and don't be reckless. Take it easy in the beginning.

As hard as I currently train, I do *not* live by the philosophy "No pain, no gain." Pain just means you went too hard and now you have to wait until you those muscles fully recover until you can work them again. Don't think that if you go too hard, you'll just exercise those muscles again. Just don't, until the pain is gone totally so your muscles can recover.

Recovery is the building phase, and they will never optimally grow unless you let them. Your best option in the beginning is to take it easy and ramp it up slowly. Like I said, I train hard now, but that wasn't always the case. I started slow, using lightweights, and I still use lighter weights than most people. You have to understand that it is not about how much weight you can lift; it is about how well you can lift the weight using the proper form to isolate the muscle you are trying to train.

I have seen guys at the gym, all of the time, using weights they shouldn't because other people are watching. Let me liberate your sense of embarrassment and tell you what I think of other people's opinions. What other people think about me is none of my business. The only opinion that matters is my own.

Do it at your own pace the way you can do it properly. I do not give one iota of thought of what someone else thinks of me when they see me using lighter weights or when they see me in my bandana headband jogging. Everyone started somewhere, even the people that look at you funny didn't appear one day and just jump on the bench press and crank out some 250-pound sets.

Besides, anyone who makes fun of someone else who is just starting out and laughing instead of helping and correcting them is just a special kind of jerk, and they should be punched in the groin. Which leads me to the next philosophy to getting your mind right: transitioning your whole life to remove negative thoughts, ideas, and people. To replace all of these things with positivity and purpose.

TRANSITIONING

I'm going to say this for the cheap seats, so you get me. *Do not check your weight on a daily basis when you start.* You are transitioning from sedentary to healthy, and your metabolism will be so groggy that it will take a bit to fully wake up (figuratively), like a small child you just woke up in the morning. It will take some time to fully awaken, and your weight will be all over the place in the beginning. The urge to check the scale will be overwhelming; you shouldn't do it for multiple reasons.

When you transition from sedentary to active, there will be all kinds of changes happening. First, you will start feeling better and then you will start looking better. The best goal you can have is to obtain a nice look for yourself; the number on the scale will not matter.

Hey, those clothes that don't fit anymore? They didn't shrink; you got bigger, accept that. But guess what? You have the power to change that. Just like you ate and relaxed yourself into this situation you can positive your way out of it. Which leads me to the next transition you need to focus on, negativity.

Both you and others around you have been feeding your negative emotions either consciously or subconsciously. How do I know there are negative people surrounding you? If you have five friends and four of them are millionaires, the fifth one is not far behind. People tend to gravitate toward like-minded individuals, so take a look around you and find who always has that negative thing to say or suggest or just ooze out of their loser face.

Part of this transitioning is accepting you caused your situation and that you can get out of it with the right attitude. Once you adopt this attitude, the losers in your life will not be hard to find. Yes, losers, people with the shit attitude thinking the world owes them everything. Thinking they are better than they are and tell you on a constant basis, either directly or indirectly, that they are better than you. These people with these kinds of attitudes about why the world is against them and that's why they can't succeed; people who see others getting promoted with hard work and they spread the rumor that they are a boot licker or make up some other reason to dirty their name as to why they were promoted over them. You know, losers.

People who claim to be ambitious but when opportunities present themselves, they fold and come up with some excuse as to why it didn't work for them. Toxic personalities that affect every person around them with their poisonous view points and words. Losers. Take a look around, you will start to see them. A little "L" starts to form on their forehead the more you actually listen to what they have to say. Nothing is ever their fault, they didn't mess up, it was because of this or that.

Part of the transitioning is to get rid of these people. Cut them out of your life entirely, or if they are coworkers, limit your activity with them if you can and don't hang out with them outside of work. If it ever comes up, don't sugarcoat it; tell them, "I'm sorry, but I'm trying to get myself into a positive place, and you are one of the most negative people I know. I just don't want your dark clouds ruining my sunny day." They'll probably react harshly like they are the most positive person on earth and get offended. That's fine. They will not be bothering you for sure.

They will surely spread rumors about you because they are toxic and want to control everything. Who cares? You sure shouldn't if you have the right attitude. The world owes you nothing except what you earned, and if others are influenced about you because of something that someone else said without defending you, then you don't need that person either. They are just following the main loser around because they seem like the dominant personality. All they are is just the most convincing loser and are constantly recruiting others to join their plight.

If they happen to be your spouse or significant other, you need to have a serious discussion with them about negativity. You need to explain to them that you are trying to turn your life around and this is what you are doing about it. Moreover, you need to ask them to try and be supportive about it and ideally, *Boil the Frog* themselves so they can journey with you out of the land of negativity.

Especially if they are your spouse, you *need* their support. You are a team, and you need that mentality. The team is your spouse/family, your group of friends, your group of coworkers, or actually being part of an organized sports team. Coming in with the attitude that "This is what we are going to do, and I want you to join me. We can both be positive moving forward and keep each other in check if we are not." That's a team, a group with not only the knowledge of where they are going, what they are doing and have the right attitude to execute plans exactly when needed. That is the attitude of what is best for the group. This will also benefit each individual in the long run.

Each member of a team serves a specific purpose in the functionality of the team as a whole. Whether you have two members on your team or eighty, the theory is the same. Transition yourself and the others around you will most likely be onboard, and if they are not, they are not a team player, they are selfish, and they are a loser that needs to go. The transition in your mentality and transitioning your body go together. You can't have one without the other without only short-lived success. Spot your own negative behavior and the negative behavior of those around you will become so apparent there will be no doubt.

That is just part of getting your life in order and setting yourself up for success. Take as many people with you can. Having like-minded people around you only increases your chances of success. Be the person that elevates the people around them as much as possible. If you achieve, reach back down, and help that person up to the same step.

I transitioned alone, and it was a longer journey than it needed to be because I didn't include the people around me at first. I didn't fail, but I could have been successful faster with the help of others around me. You will be amazed at the people around you in each direction. Some of them were just waiting for someone else to say it to get them started. Others, the losers, will make it abundantly clear that not only will that not work, you will fail miserably and come right back to their way of thinking. Those of the people you either need to talk to or just cut out of your life.

When I started this transition at forty-four years old. I was 6'0" and 235 pounds (obese by the BMI standards at 31.9), and I wanted to get back to my "normal" weight according to BMI. That was 180 pounds. However, once I got within five pounds of that goal, I started tapering off on the cardio a bit and focused on weight training, resistance band training, and yoga. I still would go for four to five-mile runs a couple of times a week, but the focus went from dropping the weight to looking and feeling great.

So even when you transition, there will be other transitions down the road. Don't be afraid of this. You embrace change now, moreover, it is necessary to change it up so you don't get bored with what you are doing. If you're not having fun, then you are not going to be motivated on the days you just don't feel like training. I like to change up the music and go on those closed loop neighborhood adventures. Listen to some movie soundtracks and make it exciting. You feel the anticipation around every corner, just like in the movies when you think something is about to jump out at you. The very way the sounds make the movie exciting can make your walk exciting.

The number 1 thing you need to accept is that you put yourself in this position with your thoughts and actions. I will continue to browbeat this into you until you get that ideology firmly in your mind. Transitioning involves understanding that your daily habits and routines are what got you here and changing these is what is going to get you out of it.

Transitioning to a healthy lifestyle will take some time, but little by little is the main focus of *Boil the Frog*. Transitioning is all-encompassing; it will affect every aspect of your life. Doing so, however, is entirely necessary to save your life.

Yes, I said save your life because whatever caused this behavior, deep down, you knew that you were slowly killing yourself. Either consciously or subconsciously. Whatever you are stuck in doing right now like overeating, overdrinking, abusing drugs, smoking, you name it. That was your goal whether you knew it or not because your outlook on life had become so bleak that you figured there was no other way to happiness besides that food or that drink or that drug and you were going to do it until it killed you because you believed there was no other way. But there is, I've been down that dark thought path and found my way back, just like you will.

I figured this out over the course of those first few weeks of long walks with just my thoughts (which we will dive into in in detail in later chapters). I was drinking ten to fourteen beers a night, sometimes, on a work night. I would stay up until 1:00 a.m. drinking and get up at 5:00 to 6:00 a.m. for work, or I would just turn off the alarm clock and just show up whenever my hangover would allow me and cost myself money.

Out there in the world, under the open sky, you just feel exposed. You look up at the sky and see the clouds moving by, and you begin to understand you are part of an entire ecosystem, an entire planet. We are all here together on this little planet, and past that is this infinite space that we know virtually nothing about! It makes you think a lot more that you would imagine once you are away from all the distractions we have come to love. Our phones, our TV, our games, all of it. You get out there and things you've been pushing down just come bubbling up and you have to deal with them.

I'd come to the realization that I had become a horrible human being. A bad father, a bad husband, and just a nasty person to be around, a monster. Even now writing about it causes some emotions to well up. Sure, I was beat up by the world, but I used to be so nice until the world made fun of me for it, even bullied me for it. Easy target, I suppose. That's one of the realizations I made is to try and get back to the friendly joking person I was when I was a kid. To have fun again!

I finally understood being depressed and angry about things that happened years ago made no sense. Using the past as an excuse for failure had been holding me back my entire life. I realized you have to live in the moment when things actually matter. I can't change what happened before, but I can change what happens next.

The "moment of clarity" I have heard from other people finally happened to me, and I knew exactly what I needed to do. I needed to forgive my past.

FORGIVE THE PAST

Wherever you are starting, it's going to be easier just to explain exactly what I did, in what order, and why. I know most of you are already thinking who is going to be on team "walking buddies" and that's fine down the road, literally and figuratively. But not at first and there's a reason why.

How to start goes back to getting your mind right. Those figurative demons nested in your brain are what got you in this situation to begin with. They are the voices telling you that you can't and that you will fail. I started small and slowly by walking to the grocery store. Then I craved longer walks. There was something about being out there under the open sky with nothing but the sounds of the world and my own thoughts.

For the first two weeks (at least), when you really get out there and start walking more than a mile at a time, do not listen to music, do not talk on the phone, do not walk with someone else, no distractions. This time will be spent with your own thoughts, and it will start the process of changing the way you think, making realizations and understanding what you believe and why.

I spent the better part of two weekends clearing out a garden that was in our backyard. That garden was the previous owner's vision, his dream. I always looked at it as a lot of work to maintain something I didn't want, so I didn't maintain it. Eight years' worth of overgrowth I had to deal with because I didn't deal with it right away.

During all of those hours, I kept coming up with thoughts about how this related to how the mind can become overwhelmed with things because they were just not addressed. If I would have done this when we first moved in, I could have completed this in less than one weekend. However, because I let things grow unchecked, almost the entirety of one weekend was just getting the garden back to the state it was when I moved in.

There were trees growing in there, for Pete's sake! Deep-rooted as well. I pulled and pulled, and they wouldn't budge. Deep roots like bad memories that were anchored into the ground. Just like bad thoughts and memories can anchor into our mind and dominate our thoughts. The only way I could get those trees out of the ground was to cut all the roots with the shovel. I literally had to get to the root cause of the problem to remove it, just like in life.

That is what your mind is full of. Deep-rooted trees that feel they have every right to live there, so they bury themselves deep because they kept getting fed by your own negativity. Getting out into the world with nothing but your own thoughts lets you understand where these roots are and what problems they are causing. You can choose to forgive these roots and just stop feeding them, or you can cut them out entirely. This is what you are doing out there, getting to the bottom of why you feel whatever is holding you back. What is the root cause of why you want to engage in overeating or alcohol abuse or drug addiction or sex addiction. Get to that root and just chop it off. Stop feeding your negative brain trees.

Probably the most ridiculous sentence you can imagine, but remember little sayings like this to help you along the way. It is literally how this book was entitled. During my transitioning, I kept muttering it to myself when I wanted to go all in. I just said, "Chill out man. Boil the frog, you'll get there eventually."

Believe it or not, you can be reasoned with, even when you are talking to yourself. It will not be easy of course, but slow boil the frog, take it one step at a time. Some people will find it right away, others will take a while. Just keep at it, and you will start to find causes and reasons, but you just have to forgive them. You can't change it, you can only accept it and move on. If you don't, you will just keep feeding those roots, and it will make it harder and harder to remove.

Why, all of a sudden, did I decide to tackle this huge garden project all by myself? I said before the garden was the previous owner's dream. Well, my little girl's dream was to have a trampoline. I was just going to clear out the garden and live with the maintenance, I told my wife, in fact. After I initially was just cleaning up around it, I said they are really well-constructed garden boxes, and it would be difficult to remove them. After I said that, my wife reminded me that was our daughter's dream—she "wants to be a flipper."

The very moment she reminded me of that, it was over, that garden was doomed. No matter how hard it was going to be or what I had to do to make it happen, she reminded me that it would make my daughter happy, and it became a branch on my train tracks. It didn't stand a chance once I set my mind to it. My wife wanted our daughter to get her wish to "be a flipper," and after that, no other obstacles mattered. I was clearing that garden and planting grass in that area so I could install a trampoline, and I was doing it right now.

Just like the past, you need to clear out your own mental garden and take as long as necessary to complete it so you can resow that soil with things you want to grow there. No obstacles matter if you find one, solve it, and keep going. Keep this up until you can forgive your past, all of it. Things that you have done and things that have been done to you. You need to forgive it because you can't change it. Back when I said put a wall up behind you, that's why. Because it doesn't matter what happened before today, it's done. The bigger the forgiveness the better.

I know some people have been through some traumatic events. You can remember them, but you do not need to let it define you as a person, and you definitely have to forgive those or you may never recover. What ever happened before is just something that you can't change, but you can choose how you react to it and just forgive it. No matter how big the event is in your past, you are still alive, and you need to act accordingly. I know big things aren't easy to forgive, *I know it*. All the more reason to just let it go and get on with your life.

Same goes for things you have done; you can't change those either. The wall I asked you to put up in your mind is to remind you that nothing from your past can stop you making positive progress on yourself— nothing. You can't change the past, you can only change the present and the future. You can look back for cars when you cross the street, but everything else is irrelevant back there so keep moving forward.

Bring some tissues or use your spare towel with you during this process. You will dig up some things you completely forgot about or blocked out, and it will make you emotional. I've had tears running down my face while walking and running, on completely separate occasions. No, I'm not ashamed to admit that we are all born with emotions and not using all of them is what is messing some of you up—hard. It's a continual process, but you've got to tackle the big things first to get your mind right.

These initial long walks will make more strides than a therapist can do in more than a year and certainly far better than anti-depressants (I've been prescribed them and they made everything numb and hazy and that's not living). You will fully understand that the number 1 thing that has been holding you back has been you. Once you are out of your own way, you can evolve to the person you were supposed to be before the world took a big old swing upside your head at one point or the other.

You can continue this process even when you begin walking with other people or out there by yourself listening to headphones. I have had music trigger long-time forgotten memories and led me down a road that began with tears and ended in forgiveness. Music triggers all kinds of emotions and forgiving the past is a continual process that keeps going even when you get past the first "big ticket" items during your initial walks. You will find the big things right away, but the subtle thoughts that were just contributing will come up as well. Don't shy away from it; embrace it when those random thoughts show up, because it's ready to be forgiven too.

Regardless of how long you have been doing it, forgiving your past may take a very long time to complete. Just like everything else here, you will know when it's enough. Sometimes I still go out without anything with me, usually my after-dinner one-and-a half-mile slow walk through the "Y" section. Usually I catch the sunset just as it happens when I make the turn around the bend of Youngwood turn.

This is just another benefit for these initial long walks and subsequent shorter walks without any distractions is keeping up your "mental garden weeding." These undistracted walks are also unbelievably effective at problem solving.

I run a small online business called Dawn Upon, selling on Amazon. E-commerce requires adaptability and commitment to the ever-changing scenarios that are involved with running this type of business. I have left my house with problems on my mind only to return an hour or two later with viable solutions that I could put into action immediately.

Bottom line with these initial walks is to what? You got it; get your mind right, and the best way to start getting your mindset correct is by forgiving the past. Les Brown is a motivational speaker and he once said, "*Life has no limitations, except the ones you make.*" These limitations during the process of getting your mind right will reveal these limitations for what they are—excuses as to why you will fail.

Speaking of Les Brown, he has a great story about growing bamboo trees that I recommend you look up and watch. I will not do it justice copying the text down here because of the sheer belief you get by watching it and by the conviction and belief of his delivery. There is more to the video than just this, but please read the main point I'm trying to make here and please find it and watch this video; daily if you can.

> In the far east they have something that's called the Chinese bamboo tree. The Chinese bamboo tree takes five years to grow. They have to water and fertilize the ground where it is every day, and it doesn't break through the ground until the fifth year. But once it breaks through the ground, within five weeks it grows ninety feet tall.
>
> Now the question is does it grow ninety feet tall in five weeks, or five years?
>
> The answer is obvious. It grows ninety feet tall in five years. *Because if at any time, had that person stopped watering and nurturing and fertilizing that dream, that bamboo tree would've died in the ground.*

For me, this was one of those speeches and lines that just gives you chills because it is so accurate. Treat all of your dreams like this, and you will succeed. When? In five years. That's what the big goals that you have no idea how to achieve are for, long-term. No idea how to do it, but I'm going to do it in five years.

How long do you walk like this? Well, probably not five years. Walking is not a huge "impossible" goal, like a five-year goal is. But it is entirely up to you, you can take as long as you need as long as you slowly make progress. However, do this for at least two to three weeks, one to three miles at a time, and at least three times a week. Preferably every day if you have the time, for the most benefit. It's what I did.

Once you have a breakthrough or a realization on your walks with your own thoughts, you will know it. You will have no doubt. That's when you can start to really turn your whole life around and even graduate to walking and talking, listening to music or audio books, or talking with a friend either on the phone or walking with you. Just make sure your friend has also done their initial alone walks in the beginning too.

Of course, this process will help you get your mind right, but to get your body right, you need to start documenting everything you consume and burn on a daily basis, starting right now.

CALORIES

I know some of you are already asking, "Well, how do I know how many calories I'm burning?" Fair question. You can search online and figure out the average burn rate based on your height, weight, and age. I don't like that. I want to know exactly what I am burning so I can know how many calories I have to limit myself to. I decided to invest in my health and buy a device that tracks my burn rate for me.

I personally purchased a Fitbit, but I saw several less costly versions are out now. I only bought the Fitbit because it was on sale, but so glad I did. I am not being compensated at all for mentioning them, for your information. I'm just telling you what I used, please feel free to find the device that best works for you, or you can use averages like I mentioned. As long as you are producing results, just keep up what you are doing.

While waiting for the actual device to arrive in the mail, I downloaded the Fitbit app so I could get familiar with its functions and features. It gives you an average burn rate for calories if it doesn't get any information from the actual device, and I knew it was slow for me, but I abided by it anyway until it arrived in the mail and kept my calories below the estimated burn rate.

I personally can't say enough about the Fitbit or similar devices and how vital it is for you if you know what your metabolic rate is and how much calories you are actually burning each day. It even tracks your sleep and lets you know what stages you were in all night. It calculates your resting heart rate, which is something everyone should know.

You can use apps to set your daily goals including steps taken, calories burned, floors climbed, miles walked, and heart zone minutes. You can customize it to fit your needs, and it is vital for goal-setting to keep you motivated. It also works best with a smart scale that can sync with an app. You can track your body weight fat percentage, bone density, muscle mass, etc. Very interesting to say the least, and a great use of technology to aid in weight loss.

There are multiple options out there for tracking for any budget. You don't need to buy all the top-of-the-line stuff that I did, as long as what you are doing is keeping you motivated, and you are sure that you are burning more than you are taking in it shouldn't be an issue.

Others don't want to track at all! They just go blind and hope for results. I personally like to know exactly how my efforts are translating in transforming my body. That's your choice! Just like everything else. I will go deeper into how these technologies can help you later in the book.

CALORIE INTAKE/
BURN RATIO

Weight loss is a math problem, nothing more. I have had people laugh in my face when I said this, and I responded with "my sixty pounds down begs to differ." I am not talking about getting shredded and getting down to 1 to 3 percent body fat like body builders, I mean general weigh loss. If you burn more calories than your intake, you will lose weight. There's no secret, no cutting out this type of food, eating more of this type of food. All those diets are just fads, and they only seem to work, for most, temporarily. Someone's way of trying to get people to try their program above another.

You can absolutely use those programs as long as they work for you. Everybody is different, and if it works, then do it! That's the whole point of the simplicity of this ideology is that each person can try anything they want because there is no one system that works for everyone. You have to find what works for you, and it has to be something that you can keep up with and not quit on, and something you look forward to. Something you enjoy, because if you don't enjoy it, you'll just quit.

Walking is it for some people, running for others. Weight training for some, yoga for others. Muscle building for some, low-impact aerobics for others. Personally, I do all of these things because they *all* have their benefits. Running and walking have cardio and fat-burning effects. Weight training helps with your overall look on the outside and overall strength. Yoga helps stretch out all those exerted muscles and help prevent injuries by stretching them out before you even use them.

I believe that's why most people fail is that they try one program, and it doesn't work for them because either they didn't get results right away (instant gratification people) or they didn't have any fun! The entire time they were focused on one thing when ultimately all things work together, not just one thing. That's the part of the fun is figuring out exactly what works for you because there is no one else like you!

This goes back to mindset and getting your mind out of the ideology that someone else put you in this condition. You did this. You put yourself in this position and you are going to have to put in the work to get out of it. My all-time favorite quote from Dr. Phil, *"You're fat. Don't sugarcoat it because you'll eat that too."*

The limits you are setting in your own mind have real-world effects on yourself. "I have insulin resistance;" "I have type 2 diabetes;" "I'm too heavy to walk." BS. Everyone can do some form of exercise. Your body is the result of your effort. If you are not getting the results you wanted yet, then you need to put in more effort to make it happen. If you are not willing to put in that work, you skipped some steps before and need to go back to the beginning.

These types of conditions are absolutely combatted by doing exactly what I am saying to do. It is physically impossible to burn more calories than you take in and not lose weight. Period. Anyone who tells you otherwise is feeding into your excuses because they failed and want to make sure you fail to justify their failure.

Would you believe it if I told you I *still* eat whatever I want? Also had people laugh in my face for this, but it's true. Pizza is my favorite food, and I didn't cut it out at all. If I have it, I make sure to leave enough room in my calorie goals to make sure I am burning far more than I take in. This is an extra mile, extra sets, anything you can do. If you want to eat what you want, you have to compensate those extra calories by either eating less of something else or working more.

I can prove it's a math problem. I did it in the real world in the worst possible conditions. In September of 2021, during an offshore stint, I contracted COVID-19. I was stuck in a hotel room from September 17 to October 4, 2021. During that time, I only had access to fast food and take out menus. Keep in mind that I was literally sick with COVID. I was symptomatic; I was not just trapped in there, I wasn't feeling well for about four to five days.

After that initial few days, I did feel better, but I could not leave the room. How much weight do you think I gained during that time just sitting around eating fast food and watching TV all day? None. In fact, I lost weight. I looked up the nutritional facts on all the foods I was eating, and I kept count. I still maintained a negative caloric intake and lost weight *eating nothing but fast food*! Sometimes I had to cut things in half and eat them again later to make my calorie goals, but that's all I did.

That hotel room was exactly twelve steps wide. I counted it many times over almost three weeks. After the initial symptomatic period, I *still* got my ten thousand steps per day, twelve steps at a time. It's about commitment. It's not about what kind of food you eat; it's about caloric intake, and your own metabolic rate, which you can increase with an active lifestyle.

For some of you, this will be an unbelievable eye-opener. Once I started keeping track of my calories, I was amazed how much more calories I was eating than I was burning. No wonder I put on so much weight. I was eating 1,200-calorie lunches while sitting at my desk job. That's 60 percent of my entire day for a 2,000-calorie diet. Now if I have a 500-calorie lunch, it's a full meal for me, and I feel stuffed. That's another worry most feel is that they will be starving by cutting out all those calories. Your body will fully adapt to the new lifestyle eventually, but in the meantime, that is literally why they invented snacks.

There are countless low-calorie snack options to get you through the initial hunger as your body begins to take from your fat stores and muscle mass. I have a low-calorie snack (100 calories or less) in between each major meal, and it really gets you through to the next meal. Is it a discipline? For sure. But it's not "impossible." If you want to be healthy and have a better body, it takes sacrifice. As long as you boil the frog and make small strides each day, you can get there!

On the day I decided to make a change in my life, I went from 235 pounds on May 1, 2021 to meeting my weight loss goal, exceeding it in fact, on October 5, 2021 (my ten-year wedding anniversary and yes, the day after I got out of my COVID quarantine eating fast food for almost every meal), weighing 175 pounds. Sixty pounds down in five months on pure diet and exercise. Just by monitoring my calorie intake and making sure I was burning more than I was taking in. No fancy program, no fad diet, no weight loss pills, just boiling the frog, eating anything I wanted.

STRETCH IT OUT!

The absolute most important part to exercising your body is to properly stretch before any exercise and preferably after as well. For a while, I attended yoga frequently, and while I recommend it for anyone, you don't have to go to a yoga class. You can search the moves and positions online and do them at home if you really wish.

Using what my yoga experience taught me, I go through a barrage of stretches before exercising. I usually mix in back and ab workouts during my "stretching" period. It lasts about thirty minutes of just stretching my entire body using a combination of yoga positions and old-school Navy stretching the military taught me.

As always, find what works for you. After a few days of working out, you are going to figure out what is sore and what you should have stretched prior to the workout. I used to focus on specific muscle groups depending on what I was working out that day. Now I do full-body workouts so my thirty minutes of stretching mixed with superman poses for the lower back and scissor kicks and crunches for my abs may be excessive for those starting out for sure.

The main focus is to properly stretch to avoid injury and reduce soreness the next couple of days. Since I'm over the hill, I also like to take a bath/steam shower combination and that really helps with reducing the soreness. I have that in my house, so may not be available to all, just letting you know all that I do.

My stretching regimen is long, since I'm over forty, to make sure I don't injure myself and more importantly, don't have to take time off from exercising to heal. I'm sore anyway, whether I work out or not, so this regimen may be over the top for someone younger, but again, find what works for you. Hold all of these stretches as long as it feels good. If something is sore and the stretch you are doing feels particularly good, hold it! Listen to what your body wants, and it will be grateful.

- Reach for the Sky
  - o First thing I always do is reach straight up trying to make the distance between my fingers reaching up and my toes pointing down become as far apart as possible. I usually do this stretch by reaching up to the cross-beam support across my garage. That way I can reach up and use the beam to brace myself and arch my back as well.
- Side and Arm Stretch
  - o One at a time, lift your arm up over your head, and let the forearm fall to the opposite shoulder. Take the opposite hand and grab above your elbow and pull toward opposite shoulder. My goal of this stretch is not just stretching the shoulder and triceps but to stretch those and the entire side of my rib cage. Pull your hips toward the side being stretched, and you should feel stretching on your entire side as well as your arm.
- Tree and King Dancer Pose Modified Combination
  - o A yoga pose that I have adapted to do without the hand on the chest. Get a solid base on your plant leg and lift the opposite foot toward your belly button with your toes pointing upward; this will fold your leg onto itself. Then tilt your leg toward behind you and really feel it stretching the hip that is off the ground.
  - o Without touching the ground, bring your foot back down and keep moving it backward until you can grab it with the same side arm (I like to whip it back there so I can grab it easy) and pull it backward while simultaneously moving your opposite arm forward like you are pointing. This will be a balancing pose as you will tilt your torso forward to be as level with the ground as possible. Reach as far forward with the

pointing arm as possible while pulling backward on your leg. This will be difficult for a beginner, but with practice you will find your balance and be able to hold this pose.

- Neck and Trap Stretch
  - o Move your right leg behind your left leg, and bend it upward so you can grab it with your left hand. Use your right hand to balance on a nearby wall equivalent. Hold your leg just above the ankle and tilt your head and neck away from the leg. You will feel a pulling from your neck through your shoulders. Once stretched to your satisfaction, switch all and do the other side.
- Shoulder stretch.
  - o Just stand with feet hip-width apart and put your right arm in front of you across the front of your body. Using your opposite arm, tuck the crossed arm into the elbow of the left arm just above the elbow of the right arm and pull and twist your body to the left. Switch and do perform the same with the opposite arms.
- Toe Touch
  - o Keep your feet hip width apart and bend over and touch both toes and hold. Keep your knees straight and reach down as far as you can. If you can't touch your toes now, it's okay. You will continue to improve your flexibility as you continue stretching and will be able to reach the floor eventually.
- Calf Stretch
  - o Keeping your right foot flat on the floor behind you, step forward with your opposite foot until you feel a distinct stretching in your calf. Some can do this while remaining standing up. I have to have my body in an arch push up position and keep my non-stretching calf foot on the heel of the stretching foot. Very much like a downward facing dog, but I have my foot on the other foot to keep it flat.

- Upward-Facing Dog
  - o Lay face down on your mat or the floor and push upward with your arms keeping your hips on the floor and tilt your head back to the ceiling. This will stretch both hips and your back.
- Isolated Hip Stretch Combination
  - o Still laying down, move your right thigh up as far toward your shoulder as you can on the same side and lift up with your arms. This is will isolate the left hip. Lift upward as far as your hip will allow. This distance will increase over time.
  - o In the same position, this time, put your foot flat on the ground and lift upward and roll sideways stretching your hip at multiple angles. You will also feel this on the side of your torso.
  - o Repeat with the opposite hip.
- Locust Pose Modified
  - o Lying flat on your stomach with your arms stretched outward above your shoulders at a forty-five-degree angle, lift your arms and legs off of the mat at the same time and raise them as high as you can and hold for thirty seconds to one minute or as long as you can.
- Superman
  - o Using the same principle as the locust pose, put your arms straight out in front of you and lift them up with your legs leaving only your belly on the mat. Do an old-school Superman flight regimen and pretend you are flying through the air doing superhero things. I change positions with my arms and lean my body side to side. Sometimes both arms in front, sometimes I change to just one. Constantly move your arms forward and backward like you are really flying and hold it as long as you can. It's a great isometric lower back workout.
- Stretch Armstrong
  - o Lying down on your left side, stretch your right arm and right leg apart, trying to get your fingertips and

toes as far apart as possible. This is a great hip flexor stretch you can really feel, hold as long as needed.

o   Flip over and repeat laying on your right side.

- Hip Scrunch
  o   Lying flat on your back, lift your right leg and bend it so your knees is resting on your chest. Pull toward your shoulders.
  o   Repeat on both sides.
- Laying Toe Touch
  o   In a seated position, keep your legs straight on the floor and stretched out in front of you as you reach your right hand to your right toe. Hold straight and lean back until you are lying flat on your back and stretch.
  o   Repeat on left side.
- Kickboxer Stretch
  o   If you've never watched the Jean-Claude van Damme movie, *Kickboxer*, you may not know what I am talking about, but if you have you will know exactly what I mean.
  o   Same as the Laying Toe Touch; however, you grab both feet at the same time and lay down with both in your hands.
  o   Take both feet and spread them as far apart as you can while holding on to them.
  o   The goal is to try and do the splits.
    - I am currently only about at a forty-five-degree angle, but the goal is to be like the movie and stretch them completely straight and be able to do the splits.
- Groin Stretch
  o   In a seated position, but both feet together, sole to sole, in front of you. Move your heels as close as you can and still be able to stretch comfortably. Grab each foot with each hand and pull toward yourself while

pushing your knees downward toward the floor. Repeat if necessary.

- Shoulder Stand
  - o Keeping your head and neck supported flat on the ground, lift both legs and grab your hips while your elbows are on the ground. Make your legs stick as high and as straight up as possible.
- Knee to the Face (not really)
  - o While in the shoulder stand, slowly move your feet backward until you can't do it anymore or your feet touch the floor with your knees just above your face.
  - o Be very careful in this pose or skip it if you are not comfortable. You have to go really slow to ensure you do not cause damage to the neck.
- Scissor Kicks and Casper Punches
  - o Lay flat on your back and keep your butt on the ground while you lift your arms and legs just high enough off the floor for movement.
  - o Alternate your legs and begin kicking in a small motion moving up and down and staying off of the floor.
  - o Simultaneously, air punch toward your knees on the opposite arm. If you are kicking with your left leg you right arm should be trying to punch your left knee. As well as the opposite, kick the right leg and try and punch your left knee, but don't actually punch it of course.
  - o This is a tremendous hip flexor and ab workout. Do this until failure.
- Suspended Crunches
  - o Lift your arms above your head and lift your legs just off the ground. Move your arms to your sides while you move your legs to do a ninety-degree bend and then kick your feet away from you while moving your arms above the head to counter balance and repeat this motion until failure.

- Flip back to your belly and repeat only the Back and Abs exercises two more times.
  o The remaining stretches will focus on stretching those muscles you just worked out.
- Upward Bow (very advanced)
  o Laying down flat, put your hands on the floor just above your shoulders.
  o Thrust your hips up and push with your arms.
  o This will put you with your hands and feet on the floor and arch your whole back.
  o This takes some strength so this may actually be a goal for some of you to actually complete this stretch properly. I know it was for me and was very excited when I was actually able to do it, so be careful here as well.
- Cat Pose
  o With hands and knees on the floor and your head down and back arched upward, stretch your back toward the ceiling
- Cow Pose
  o With hands and knees on the floor, lift your head toward the ceiling and arch your back downward, stretch your back down and your head up.
- Child's Pose
  o Put your knees and pelvis as low to the floor as possible and stretch out your arms as far in front of you as possible. You are focusing on stretching the lower back and the mid to upper muscles just behind your shoulder blades.
- Downward Face Dog/Hand Walk Up
  o After the child's pose, I will use my hands to walk upward to give a final back stretch before standing up and beginning either my weight training or my run.

Some of these poses can be advanced for beginners, especially for long-time sedentary beginners, so just be careful and do them the best you can. Obviously, I made up some of the names—right now, in fact—because I just do them, I didn't need to name them. So that was fun, except for the ones I just looked up because they are basically yoga poses that I modified slightly. You can search online for the ones that I used their actual names or look online for a regular stretching routine. Plenty of content out there for you to find the right ones. If you already have an ailment, like a sore back, lots of content on how to specifically target almost any muscles with stretches.

Regardless, you can pick and choose what works for you and add your own. This is extensive, but I don't get injuries from workouts anymore either, so just use these carefully, and as you need, and you should be fine.

Embrace the suck!
—Standard Yogi Phrase

BURN THOSE CALORIES

**Please make sure you check with a physician prior to starting any workout program. Please make sure you don't have an undiagnosed condition before starting. Also to make sure that you are physically able to start an exercise regimen.

As inspiring as I can be, I inspired my friend Randy to get back into shape. I mentioned him before, but I'm going to delve more into it as an example of what not to do. Randy's problem was he was over sixty and hadn't worked out for years. Unfortunately, he didn't have the benefit you all have of reading this book.

He joined a gym and got a free training session with a "fitness trainer." I put that title in quotes because once he told me what he did on his first day with that "trainer," I had to put it in quotes. That incompetent trainer put him through the ringer on Day 1. The man could barely walk down a hill, he was so sore. It put him out of commission to go back for at least a week.

This is where boiling the frog really comes into play, especially when it comes to starting in a gym, (which I do not recommend to start there). You have your mind right, you are motivated, you are ready to go. You hit the gym or you walk around and watch what other people are doing and you work out hard. You are going to melt those pounds off today! Problem with that is you are going to hit it as hard as that fitness trainer hit my buddy Randy and you're not going to physically *able* to exercise for the rest of the week because of the pain.

Slowly! You build up your exercises slowly. If you choose to start at the gym, your first two to three weeks at the gym should feel like waste of time. Those quick twenty- to thirty-minute light exercises are not a waste of time, but they may feel like that is the case. You are slowly acclimating your body for the stress you are about to put it through in the following months.

Not just the gym, walking too! Before you build up to those mind-repairing long walks, you need to boil the frog and take it slow, or the damn thing is going to jump out of the pot, and you'll be back to square one. Meaning if you go too hard too fast, it will *not* be fun, you will *not* enjoy it, and you will most likely end up quitting.

Have a plan and know that you are not stopping how you start, you are continuously increasing your exercises with more time, more distance, more reps, more sets, etc. But do so slowly, if you start with a twenty-minute walk on the treadmill, go twenty-one the next time, or increase the pace by 0.02 mph—just something extra that you know you can handle.

You know where you are weak and what you need to focus on, but build it slowly. You should always have a plan of action when you walk into that gym or down that street. My weakest areas are pull-ups and bench presses, so guess what I do the most of? Correct, both of those. No matter what I work out on any given day, those two exercises are always part of it. I may skip body parts that are either sore or I just don't have time that day, but those never get skipped because those are where I am weaker and what I need to focus on.

I can't even do regular pull-ups right now! I have to use a bar I put inside a door frame and give myself a jump up to get over the bar every time. You will find there are just things you can't do at first, but you can use little cheater techniques to help you until you are strong enough. I used to only be able to do a couple, but now boiling the frog, I can do multiple sets of eight using this technique, and I'm ending it with regular pull-ups. So far, three is my max without jumping, but I'm sure I'll be able to crank them out like a pro by this time next year.

No matter where you are, if you are at home or the gym or out on the road, you need to have a plan before you even start and execute that plan. Especially if you are walking in potentially dangerous areas either from the traffic or from high-crime areas. Moreover, once you start running, you run the same path so you can start to see your progress in the pace you run at and in your total time, which is really motivating.

I used to go to gyms, and every January and February, the gym was flooded with novice exercisers fulfilling their new year's resolutions. Slowly but surely, the same faces I saw before the first of the year ended up being the same faces I saw again after the resolution people gave it up. Every one of them came in there to do their resolution, and 99 percent of them I never saw again because they had no plan.

When March came around, I made it a point of going around to all new people I saw that were still there and gave them all the pointers I could after congratulating them for making it this far and to encourage them not to give up.

I speak a lot of harsh words that people don't want to hear, but I always want you to succeed. Telling you all that I'm sure some of you will fail is just the reality of things because it's true, people just give up when things get hard. Only the truly committed will make it through the initial gauntlet you have to run to get into the active lifestyle mode you need to be in to get into a good mental and physical health category.

Point being, build your exercises slowly. Increase slow over time. Until you are in an optimal weight and health standpoint, you shouldn't do any exercising that you cannot speak conversationally without difficulty. You should be able to have a conversation during these exercises, easily. Once you reach your health goals, which can mean your weight goals, you can get into the running and heavy weight training to build cardio health and muscle.

I took about three to four months of steady walking before I felt the urge to pick up the pace and take off running. I didn't get very far, but I was excited that I felt like doing it, I'm sure you will to. You will know when you are ready, don't hold back; just take off. Once you are out of breath or get a stich in your side or just don't feel right, you need to stop running and start to walk again, but don't stop entirely. Keep moving, keep walking even when you stop running and wait to catch your breath. When you feel better and still have time/distance left, take off again. Rinse and repeat.

Keep doing this slowly over time, and eventually, you can run your whole course. My first course was 4.5 miles, and I slowly increased the pace up to a ten-minute mile pace and did not stop the whole time. But that nowhere near happened over night. It took me over four months to get there.

That may be fast for some and slow for others, but my pace does not matter to you. Because you have control of your own progression. No one knows your body better than you and how you feel. Only you can turn up the heat on your frog slowly enough to keep it in the pot. If you overdid it? Take the time off to recuperate, this is literally your own pace for a reason, so you can succeed.

When you begin, you may feel like it's a waste of time, but that slow acclimation will pay off big time. I myself have overdone it in the past and put myself out of commission for up to a month waiting on a strain to heal. Every time you do that, it's like starting over, so remember, slow and steady wins the race. I constantly remind myself, you should be "coasting." You can think of your own phrases to tell yourself, but that's my favorite, other than "boil the frog," of course. When I catch myself picking up the pace too much and panting, I remind myself I should be coasting, I should be slow boiling that frog.

A NEW BEGINNING

I wrote this book to give the ideals, principles, and strategies that I used a name and a purpose. I was going to include a much larger section about myself in the middle, but I wanted you all to get through the ideology from start to finish first, so you understand why I did what I did and how.

Because who am I? No one right now, as far as the world is concerned, so I found it pretty pompous to write a full section about myself when that's not why most got this book. My literal only claim to fame at this moment is sharing a birthday with the greatest quarterback of all time, Tom Brady (August 3, 1977). Not much of a claim to fame if you need to use someone else. So we'll skip the credits and get straight to the action and such as that.

I only glazed over the concepts for the sake of getting through it all and understanding it before you start. The following chapters will be in addition to and double-down the concepts I spoke of in the beginning of this book as well as include some more insights into myself and why I needed to do this to begin with.

If you already started while you were reading, that is certainly fine too, and I applaud your motivation. Equally goes the other way, I like to read books as a whole before taking any action, so that's fine too. As long as action is taken, it's your pace and your program. Complete it the best way you know how to ensure you will succeed.

Now that you have read this far, you should understand that I can take you through a step-by-step process on exactly what I did that you could follow and get the same results. I'm going to show you exactly what you need to do to match my weight loss and get healthy. You will literally have no excuse. I'm basically giving you an address, you're putting it in your GPS, and following what it's telling you to do, and you will lose the weight you want. It's that simple of a concept, but it's a harder road to actually walk. Both literally and figuratively.

Next, I will take you through my thought process and how I got started. Again, though, I can show you the road to take, but you are the one who has to walk down that path. You don't have to do it alone; I did eventually, but I didn't start alone, that's for sure.

FOR STARTERS

I went for a walk with a couple of coworkers after being stuck on a ship for several months. It was nice to just be able to go for a walk after you have been stuck on a ship that is only 128 feet long. So, walking to the end of the pier and back about a mile away was pretty appealing. You could say that I literally started my journey out of boredom and cabin fever.

Somewhere in that walk, I made a decision that when I went back home, I was going to start walking more. I kept hearing ten thousand steps is a good goal. The ten thousand steps concept is that this extra exercise of the ten thousand steps per day would cause most people to lose one to one and a half pounds per week. Which is a good pace especially if you have a lot extra.

I, for sure, didn't reach that goal right away, purely out of embarrassment. Anyone else here just not work out because they were embarrassed? I'm sure there's a couple people here that feel that way. I don't know why, but telling my wife I was going to walk to the store was like announcing I was trying to get into shape. Then you go to do it and you start thinking, *Well, what if I fail? I'd be embarrassed to make a big deal about getting back into shape only to quit a month later.*

Ironically, it was this first statement, "I'm just going to walk to the store. I'm not getting much," started my accountability. Once I made that statement, I knew from then on I was on the hook. Her opinion matters to me so she's the one I wanted to tell first. She was the motivation I needed.

For you, it can be anything or anybody. For most people, it's putting it out there on social media, which I highly encourage everyone to do. It's not about bragging, it's about sharing your goals. You should post a *#day1* post when you start to start your accountability which is everything you need to achieve. Accountability to yourself mostly, but when you share it, discuss it with other people, they will not only encourage you, but they may even join you, and you become each other's motivation to get out there because sometimes you won't feel like it.

Once you get over that initial hump, it becomes easier. It's basically finally admitting to someone other than yourself that you do have a problem and you are going to start working on it. That can be embarrassing, but get over it, it's pointless. It's a big deal in your mind, but to others, they'll be like, "Okay, go ahead. Whatever."

Start small, but let others know you are beginning. That is the best way to get started is to put yourself on the hook to yourself. Your opinion in this journey is the only one that matters because you are the only opponent you will face…unless you run into mean dogs, which I have. Which brings me to safety before you start.

As always, please, please, please, get a check up with a licensed physician prior to starting exercise and diet changes. You may have a condition you do not know about which may require you to change your diet anyway. Let your doctor know that you are establishing a baseline because you are going to begin an exercise and diet regiment. They should give you a full physical and do blood work to check for conditions you may have. Small price to pay.

One of the bedrock philosophies of this ideology is that you can still eat what you want, just not as much as you want, does not apply when you have a medical condition that says otherwise. Please do not take what I am saying as a free license to disregard medical recommendations, that is not what I am advocating. I am teaching that you do not have to give up any of the foods you are medically allowed to have to lose weight.

The old saying was right. Action conquers fear. With the embarrassment finally out of the way, I began my long journey with a 0.75 walk to a grocery store to pick up some bread, feeling like I was embarrassed to be embarrassed. It's just a walk; don't know why that was embarrassing, but here we are. With the embarrassment of the notion all gone now, a few days later, I walked again to a store farther away, almost a full mile.

I walk at a pace that will produce about two thousand steps per mile, so a roundtrip to a store almost a mile away got me 40 percent to my goal, and I had a small stash of groceries as isometric weights for my walk back. A few times I would use a larger bag that was strong and swing the bag around as I walked back. Mostly just to have some fun, and secondly, it's great for safety as cars will definitely notice a maniac walking down the street swinging a bag around like an idiot, and thirdly, it adds to your calorie burn. It's a great shoulder/arm workout to swing it back and forth in big arcs periodically or alternately switching arms. You are basically triple dipping: getting groceries, burning fat, and exercising your arms and legs all at the same time! (Just make sure you have a really strong bag.)

These periodic walks to the store are such a great way to start out. They are the embodiment of boil the frog because of how quick they are, and you get a small break in the middle when you shop. They also avoid the mistake most new exercisers run into which is overdoing it. Unless you are nowhere near a store, then that would not be ideal. You should start with half- to one-mile walks and take your cell phone for safety reasons and in case it starts raining/storming, or you injure yourself, but stay off of it, please.

I mention safety a lot. Like I said, it's a cars world, and we are just walking in it. But cars are not the only thing to look out for out there. Depending on where you live, there may be dangerous animals out there; I know I run into loose dogs more often than I care to. Only one very small dog ever took a nip at me and barely left a scratch, but you will run into overzealous pets for sure that got out or ran away from their homes and are lost and confused.

I carry a retractable baton with me when I walk. I've only ever came close to pulling it out once. That was an older-looking pit bull that seemed friendly, but I just kept my hand out in front of me and kept her away just by backing up. If you ever encounter an animal, it's best to try and remain calm and just keep them in your eye line in front of you, even if you are going the other way, back away slowly.

They will usually understand that you are not interested in some dog love and will lose interest.

Be safe out there. There is no reason to be unprepared even when you are trying to exercise. I don't walk there, but I work near a place that the president of the company I worked for went to walk for lunch and was attacked by a group of kids playing the "knock-out game." Smaller individuals, I would recommend carrying some pepper spray or perhaps a stun gun. Basically, I would rather have something and not need it than need something and not have it.

Also, once you graduate to running, if you see a dog break their leash to get you or get out in anyway to chase you, just stop. Stop cold, and usually they have no idea what to do. But if you keep running or run faster, they think it's a game and will try and get you. But I digress.

If you don't have a store close you, you'll need to sort out a route to take to get your initial walking engine started. If you have been a very sedentary person and have a lot of weight to lose, just start with the example starting goal plan earlier. It doesn't matter where you start as long as you continually make progress and beat your best from yesterday.

Your body will let you know if you did too much, especially the next day and the day after that. When you begin your walks, don't try for ten thousand steps; try to walk around the block if you are on one or to the end of your driveway and back if it's long enough. The next day will tell you if it was too far. If you are sore, then wait until it's gone and do it again. That is the same principle and measuring stick I use any time I accelerate my workouts.

Once you start something new, do that workout, wait until the pain is gone, and do it again. Eventually, you will not have pain and you can step it up again. Of course, the opposite is also true, if you do a workout and there was *no* pain the next day or the day after that, then step it up a little bit. Like I said, it should feel like a waste of time when you first start. That is how your body will slowly adapt from a sedentary to an active lifestyle.

Slowly stepping up is how I lost sixty pounds in five months. As I type right now, I pushed a little too hard last week, made my shoulder sore, so now this is a cardio/stretching/yoga/resistance band week until I recover. No pain no gain is a philosophy, but not a very good one. Yes, you will have pain when you begin, but you don't need the pain to actually gain muscle function and growth. If you slowly step it up, you can have muscle gains without the pains while losing fat.

So first steps will seem pointless, but your initial goal when beginning your steps is to find your starting point. Some people are in better or worse shape than they think, and it will be a shock to them, but you have to find your baseline so you can begin building your foundation of healthy habits that will change your life.

MY STANCE ON DOUBTERS OF MY TACTICS

I'm going to anticipate here with the gloves off because I have already heard these. I have no doubt that I will have my fair share of critics and naysayers because I already do just in casually speaking to people about it. I am not only standing by what I am teaching, *I actually did it* this way and lost sixty pounds and got down to 12 percent body fat doing nothing but this, so you got nothin' on me. You can follow what I did and get results or argue that it doesn't work without trying it because you're a lazy piece of crap and expect to fail.

> *If you think you can do a thing or think you can't do a thing, you're right.*
> —Henry Ford

I've already heard it from some people just discussing this philosophy online and in person. Needless to say, all of those people were overweight. "It doesn't work that way;" "People have insulin resistance and can't lose weight;" "There's better ways to lose weight than that;" and I'm sure there will be a myriad of other quotes from equally fat people.

Is it taboo to call someone fat? I don't care, I used to be one, so I know all of your excuses and reasons why you can't exercise. Do you know what I hear? "Blah blah blah, it's too hard." If you want a stepped-up body, you have to step up your efforts.

If you want to chalk it up to me just having outstanding discipline and exercise ethic, fine. But I did exactly what I am telling you to do, and it worked. No one can argue that fact.

With that being said, I will also say that I will agree that eating whatever you want is *not* ideal for losing weight. However, it is a method people will actually use because it's not a matter of eating things you don't like to lose weight, it's just a matter of tracking those calories and burning more than you eat.

Could I have lost weight faster if I would have just changed my diet? Sure, I could have, but you have to take into account people and their attitude toward unpleasant things. In my opinion, you can't continue to do something if you are not enjoying it without either giving it up or going insane.

Final stance on arguments if you disagree with my tactics: find your own damn tactics then. If you are not part of the solution, you are part of the problem. Either step up or shut up. Naysaying someone else's dreams to justify your own failures just makes you a piece of crap. Period. Moving on.

IT ALL BEGINS
WITH MINDSET

Ironically, my weight loss and change in my life philosophy had nothing to do with weight. I started an Amazon FBA business with the brand Dawn Upon selling outdoor and fishing gear. I signed up with a group called Nine University. Their program walks you through how to become an Amazon seller, and in the beginning, they recommended I read a book to get my mind in the right place to succeed. Sound familiar? Yup, I absolutely adopted it and it changed my life permanently.

Mindset: The New Psychology of Success by Dr. Carol S. Dweck was what my motivation coach recommended I read. I did so over a few weeks while operating on a ship offshore and reading it little by little before going to bed. It is not that long of a book, only 320 pages, and it repeats the same principles and ideology a lot (also sound familiar?), so it really rams it home with all sorts of real-life examples. A lot of that page count is a big reference section in the back as well.

The book was written by a psychologist, so I don't know if she used some mind meld magic or not, but all I can say is about two to three months after I read it, the seeds they planted into my fertile mind grew and toggled some off switch to on or hit the "go baby go" button, and I have been changed ever since. I recommend this book to everyone I meet, to everyone I know, and I do so at great length. I'm sure a few people are tired of hearing it, but those people still haven't read it, so there you go.

It is not a mystery what this book is telling you, but it tells you in a way that somehow rewires how you see what's going on around you and in your life. Almost like what happened in the movie *Limitless* where Bradley Cooper's character looks around his pigsty of an apartment and is disgusted at the sight (without any magic and dangerous pills, of course). His new way of thinking made him realize what he was doing and how he was living and immediately cleaned his whole apartment that had been neglected for months. Whatever happened, it set me on fire and haven't been able to stop moving forward since.

The best way I can describe it is the old saying, "Anything worth doing is worth doing right." It removed my laziness and replaced it with motivation. You see what needs to be done and you do it and you do it right. No cutting corners, no "I'll do it next time," no putting things off. You see something, you do it, even if you are in the middle of doing something else.

So now that I had this new mindset to see the wrong thing and fix it what was first thing I saw? That I had become a fat, lazy, piece of crap that waited so long to buy new pants that I bought the size above them and they were still tight.

I see that I drank too much because I was dissatisfied with the life I myself had created. Nothing is more pathetic. Your life is crap because you caused it and to get through it you have to drink anywhere between eight to fourteen beers every night just to get through your own disappointment in yourself.

Worse off, for *no* reason, all of it was in my own head. My family did nothing wrong. I just blamed everyone else for everything instead of looking at myself. I have a beautiful "trophy wife" and an amazing (but stubborn) and equally as beautiful daughter (thankfully takes after her mother). I was basically getting paid to do very little until I went offshore for work. I had a decent life, but I was depressed because I was unfulfilled, it wasn't whole. I never did anything worth telling anyone about, not since I left the Navy anyway.

The company I work for has no ambition about being anything but government contract holders, and when you don't work for that department, then you don't matter and just shut up about changing the culture around here. Everyone there is comfortable having no standards, and it just didn't sit well with me, even before my mindset changed. Once it did, holy crap, did I have a lot of suggestions, but again, just shut up, we like the standards bar to be set so low it makes an actual noise as it's dragged around the warehouse.

Once you develop the winner's attitude, you just see things all around you that are not up to the standard you are now setting for yourself, and it just carries over to all aspects of your life. You learn to cut off and cut out things and people that are just not good enough. You see the losers much easier and know exactly why—it's their attitude.

Oh, and you can shove your politically correct crap. There are winners and losers in life. Not everyone wins and not everyone deserves a trophy. Great effort is rewarded with great results. Saying otherwise is how we got here to this entitlement society that thinks the world owes them every damn thing. The same mentality that I myself was stuck in and snapped myself out of.

So when I say get your mind right, that is how I started. Mindset is everything, and you will most likely fail if yours is not right, and you will blame someone else for your own failure, probably me. If you do that, your mind wasn't right to begin with. Your mind is the engine, your attitude is the fuel, and the rest of the train just follows along with it helplessly pulled in whatever direction your mind sent it to go.

THE WINNER'S ATTITUDE

Winning is not a sometime thing; it's an all the time thing. You don't win once in a while; you don't do things right once in a while; you do them right all of the time. Winning is a habit. Unfortunately, so is losing.

—Vince Lombardi

Getting your mind right, making your brain understand that we don't do things half-assed, we go all the way. We do what is necessary to win, all of the time. It changes the very way you think to make every single action you do throughout the day become an accomplishment. Being active and engaged in accomplishing tasks on a daily basis is what leaves you feeling fulfilled.

We were never meant to have information at the touch of a button inside our pockets all of the time. We were never meant to pull up to a window and be able to trade money for food. We were supposed to struggle! We were supposed to hunt our meat and have to forage and gather our fruits and vegetables. We were meant to protect our young from predators.

All of these things have been made so easy for us, that we have lost our sense of daily accomplishments and it has made millions of people feel depressed. When you go into your day with the attitude that you will get things done today and you do, that feeling of accomplishment is a great feeling.

If you love your job, then think why you love it. Same for the other way around, do you hate your job? Why? I would almost guarantee that the people that love their job feel like it serves a purpose and leaves them filling fulfilled. Same guarantee will go the other way, I'm sure a lot of you feel the exact same way I do about my job, like I could leave tomorrow, and nothing would change. Nothing would matter. These are what are called soul suckers, as they just suck the life out of you doing unimaginative mundane task after mundane task with no sense of accomplishment.

If you hate your job and feel unfulfilled, there's not only good news for you, there is hope. Most of us have heard the phrase, "the world is what you make of it." Previously, I found this to be a ridiculous statement. Of course, before, I had a losing mentality. The world owed me something because I was entitled. You can't change the world, that's a ridiculous statement, I used to think.

Contrary, if you have a winner's attitude, that statement hits you right in the feels. You are full on Walter White from *Breaking Bad*, "I am awake," and understand exactly what he means when he says the phrase. The giant anvil or clarity hit you right in the head and removed the cobwebs. All of a sudden, that statement makes the most sense of anything you have ever heard. It's true, you can't change the world, but you can choose how you react to it. You have awakened, you see it all now.

You can have an unfulfilling job and not look at it like it's a boring job, but you see it as a job with the freedom to allow you to dream other things can be possible. Look up over that rut you are stuck in and see the world for what it is, a bevy of accomplishments just waiting to happen.

I had this very thought last night: *I can literally do anything I set my mind to do. It is entirely up to me to make things happen, and I can.* You control everything you do once you understand your only limits are the limits you have been programmed to set for yourself.

Society wants workers, and they need workers to function. Everything you have been exposed to since you were just old enough to go to school has been made so you do what your told and perform work when told to do so. Just think about that. Show up to school on time or there will be punishment. Don't turn in your work on time, there will be punishment. Interact when we say to interact. No talking unless you have permission.

If school was about learning actual life skills, teenagers that move out would not be surprised that television actually costs money. They would know how to do their taxes. They would know how to save money. They would understand how to question things that they don't understand; they would be critical thinkers. They would know what that means to think critically, something no one in the education system wants for people they are programming to be drones. Oh my, that is a phrase almost no employer wants their employees to do: think critically.

Just like Mr. White, you are awake; you are sane in a crazy world. So much so that the crazy people think *you* have gone crazy. You have seen behind the curtain and see the puppet strings. Your limitations have been ingrained into you so you will be a good worker.

Your attitude and habits have to always be focused on winning. You do things all the way, no cutting corners, and no shortcuts. Life is hard, you have to train hard to face it both mentally and physically. If you are soft in either, you are not winning, you are losing, every day. Each day you put off, you get deeper and deeper into that rut until you don't even realize you are in one. It is a constant game of virtual tug-of-war. If you are not pulling the rope, it's pulling you, and pulling you down.

The winner's attitude is the attitude you have when faced with obstacles and challenges and the only time on your schedule is right fricking now and your only attitude is, "Let's fricking do this." Not tomorrow, not someday. Especially not "someday." I have searched and searched and as many times as I have looked on the calendar, I have never found "someday." It is always today. Because someday is not on a damn calendar! It's a stall tactic for losers to end a conversation when winners ask them when they are going to do something.

You have to make a choice right now, are you a winner or a loser? Have you read this whole book and haven't done anything yet? Whether you have or not, get up and do something right now. I would virtually guarantee every single person reading this book has something they can do right now that they have put off. Do it. Do it right now. Act.

You have been programed your whole life to react, not act. Time to start changing things. Time to start being proactive and not reactive. Go do something right now, prove to yourself that you are a winner. Prove to yourself that you are willing to change the script you have been written into. Prove to yourself—not me, not to anyone else. Only proving to yourself will start changing your mentality. So go now, I'll wait.

INTERMISSION

(**"Girl from Ipanema" plays softly in the background**)

Welcome back. Since you all left and did something, you all should feel a sense of accomplishment. Feeling accomplished is the best cure for depression I have ever experienced. It will become addicting to have that feeling. So much so that you will begin to set challenges for yourself on a daily basis. It will start affecting every facet of your life. It will become a habit to not only get the job done but get it done the way it should be done, to do it right.

Daily accomplishments are the cure for unfulfillment. If you love your job, that's great, but most do not, and this will help tremendously. I remember when I was locked down in quarantine, I had all of the time in the world to work on this book, and I don't think I wrote more than one page. My depression for lack of daily accomplishments at that time was more powerful than my desire to win. It becomes self-feeding and lulls you to sleep and get stuck in the rut. You have to snap yourself awake and get out of it.

It took me several weeks after the quarantine to reset back into the winning mentality. To get out of the notion that I was no longer stuck in a space and was free to roam the world. Both physically and metaphorically. I was trapped in a room, but before, I was trapped in my life, so the results were the same. You need those accomplishments daily to feed the winner.

Just like the old Cherokee story:

> An old Cherokee chief was teaching his grandson about life.

He said, "A fight is going on inside me," he told the young boy. "A fight between two wolves. The Dark one is evil—he is anger, envy, sorrow, regret, greed, arrogance, self-pity, guilt, resentment, inferiority, lies, false pride, superiority, and ego."

He continued, "The Light Wolf is good—he is joy, peace, love, hope, serenity, humility, kindness, benevolence, empathy, generosity, truth, compassion, and faith. The same fight is going on inside you, grandson…and inside of every other person on the face of this earth."

The grandson ponders this for a moment and then asked, "Grandfather, which wolf will win?"

The old Cherokee smiled and simply said, "*The one you feed.*"

I can tell you unequivocally that this is an accurate statement. Having fed both metaphorical wolves in my life, I can tell you that the dark wolf will never get one scrap of food from my table ever again and the light wolf can have an unbelievably delicious Pepperoni Crazy Calzone from Little Caesar's pizza, anytime it wants. The light wolf is very powerful and can use the calories (2,560 calories to be exact).

You believe you need the dark wolf to get through life but understand that the light wolf is ten times more powerful and can handle situations even easier than the dark wolf could with way better results. You just have to be aware which wolf you are feeding and feed it all of the time.

To sum up (too late), the winner's attitude is plainly this: You understand that it is your willingness to believe you can, the limits you set for yourself can be removed, and the real limits that you face can be overcome by taking as many small steps needed to make it happen no matter how long it takes.

Like in *Star Wars* when Luke first arrives to the Dagobah system, he has a hard time landing and ends up crashing his spaceship into the swamp. Once Yoda actually agrees to train Luke to become a real Jedi he asks him to use *the Force* (telekinesis/able to move things with your mind) to get his X-Wing spaceship out of the bog. Luke tries his best and makes the ship shake but he gives up and it sinks right back down.

Shortly afterwards, Luke expresses, "You want the impossible," to Yoda in defeat. Yoda simply closes his eyes and lifts his hand. Luke turns around from the tree he was leaning on in defeat only to see that Yoda not only got the X-Wing out of the swamp, but it is currently flying its way to the shore. After Yoda sets the spaceship gently down, safe from the swamp, he simply puts his hand down and looks at Luke.

Luke says, "I can't believe it."

Yoda responds, "That is why you failed."

Believe in yourself. Understand that most "impossible" situations are just really difficult ones you haven't solved yet. All problems have a solution, and all winners can find them no matter where they are hiding. It's just a matter of time and effort. That's the winner's mentality, the tougher the challenge, the sweeter the victory.

WALKING THROUGH YOUR PAST

Walking to the store gives you a small taste of the freedoms on roaming your own neighborhood. It's a very small taste, but there is something there you can't quite pinpoint until you get into actual long walks. So instead of planning a walk to the store, I decided one evening to just stroll around my neighborhood, and what a difference. On Racetrack Road, there's always noise and traffic whizzing by, distractions at every turn.

I live in Bowie, Maryland, and it has a distinctive design style. Each neighborhood is broken up into sections, and each section is named with the same starting letter. For example, I walked to the "I" section on Idlewild Drive just down the road from my "Y" section.

Each drive in each section loops the entire section and comes back to the main road. They also have side streets and courts that branch off the main drive creating the section. Like Ivy Hill Lane and Iris Court all branch off of Idlewild Drive which just makes a big circle encompassing the entire "I" section.

Point being, these sections are perfect for walks when you are in your own thoughts. The sections are off the main road, and once you walk down the drive for a few minutes, you are in the usually peaceful serenity of neighborhood sounds. Just the sound of the world and the very rare car driving by.

Moreover, since these sections always loop back to the main road, what I did was whichever turn I came to first, I turned that way the whole time. So if you take the right fork, then you always turn right on every street, and you will end up back where you started.

This takes navigation out of your thinking and allows you to work out your mind properly.

If you look it up on the map and follow it with your finger, you can see that it is correct. If you want, follow this on the map, you can pull it up on your phone or search on your computer later.

1. Idlewild Drive to Irongate Lane and turn right.
2. Irongate Lane to Ivy Way (this is a dead end, but just walk on it until it comes back to where you started) and turn right.
3. Ivy Way loops back to Irongate Lane and turn right.
4. Irongate Lane to Irongate Lane and turn right (this also loops onto itself)
5. Irongate Lane to Idlewild Drive and turn right (this takes you back to your original right turn on Irongate).
6. Idlewild Lane all the way back to the main road.

All right turns or left turns (if you prefer to change it up), and keep the same rules. Always turn the same direction. Of course, this doesn't work everywhere. You have to look and the map and make sure until you know your neighborhoods. I used to have my phone out all of the time when I first started, now I just have my neighborhood memorized, which is also a good thing to do just in general.

You get to see and meet some of your neighbors as well. Don't forget to wave to your neighbors! Speaking of which, if you have an activity or something in the way on the Courts or the Ways, any of the streets that are dead ends, you can always skip them. I skipped Courts and Ways when I first started but wanted to add distance eventually, so I started walking them as well.

Long-winded intro, sorry, but wanted to add that info for a bit and finally found a spot to do so. Anyway…

Either preplan or go on the fly, but these initial first walks are where you catch the bug. When you cross that threshold of walking in the insanity of busy roads to the serenity of quiet neighborhoods, your whole mind opens up. Especially if you have a route like this where you are always turning right or left, you don't have much else to occupy your mind. Planning easy routes is best when you are try-ing to work out issues, forgive the past, or problem solve.

Whichever way you go walking, these first two to three weeks you need to be in your own head a couple miles at a time (one to three miles) works best at first, but you can increase slowly, boil that frog. That means no headphones, no talking on the phone, and no walking buddies yet.

The world has become a tightly packed group of people, espe-cially if you live near a major metropolitan area. We are all so close to each other that it doesn't allow you to think about yourself very much. You're looking out for traffic or other people, you're talking with other people, etc. You're always focused on the outside world, and you need to order the chaos of a busy mind. Most of that is caused by technology, so just leave your phones in your pockets.

Once you have a nice and warm fuzzy feeling and are in a good quiet and safe neighborhood or place, start thinking about your life. Think about the events that happened in your past that lead to you doing what lead you to want to change it. This is not an easy thing to do, especially if you have a very troubled past.

Again, I am not advocating to forget the past. I'm telling you to first think about it. Really think about it and think about what lead you here. If you've suffered trauma, either mental or physical, it will not be hard to find. Think about how it changed you for better or worse. Think of the resulting ripple effects through your whole life.

Relating story, I was using my pressure washer the other week-end—another one of those things I had been putting off, but putting things off is not for winners. I noticed that some areas I could just give a once over and it was clean. Others, I needed to spend more time on as they had set in deep. I kind of chuckled and thought how much like forgiving the past pressure washing is. You are cleaning away years of build up to get back to the clean shiny new looking item that is underneath it all. Just like you have built up layers to protect yourself throughout your entire life.

If you were bullied, you develop a combative and defensive atti-tude toward. everyone, I know I did—that's one layer. If you lost someone, you put another layer on to protect those feelings. All these layers we add to protect ourselves from the bad things in life also shields us from enjoying life itself, good or bad. It takes some time to strip all of that away and find who you actually are under all those layers.

It is a fundamental desire for one to figure out who they are, and it can be jarring, so you have set up your path safe enough that you can go deep in your mind. Just be sure to leave enough mind power to pay attention to where you are going. The walking tactics I discussed before that allow you to set up non-thinking navigation, like closed loop neighborhoods, are perfect for walking through your past. A long straight road is good too, but these are usually found on busy roads, so I don't recommend these at first because you will not have headphones to block it out yet.

Walk through your past, the good and the bad, and realize how it has shaped and defined you. Did it cause you to seek happiness through food? Through drinking? Through drugs? Through sex? Have you buried the pain and just let it fester? This is the worst kind of coping to shove it down. You can't fit ten pounds of crap in a five-pound bag.

Whatever happened, it didn't kill you. You are still alive and need to act accordingly. I like to repeat things that matter because that's what you need to know. It's *okay*. You can't change it; you can let it define you if you're not ready yet, but eventually you will not have to.

You can even frequently acknowledge that it's there, but you have to forgive it. Forgive yourself, forgive others, because it literally doesn't matter no matter how much you think it does. Thinking so deeply that it's impossible to let something go is exactly why you haven't yet. But you can, you can let it go. Whatever your "*it*" is, it doesn't change one thing about what you are about to do next. It has *no* power over you except the power you give it.

There's a reason I say that this tactic is far superior than talking about it with a therapist because you are the only person who knows exactly how you feel. You don't have to spend hours waiting for someone else who just met you to question their way to get to the root cause of your issues.

You are expecting them to navigate directly to your problem, but they don't have access to all your memories and experiences up to that point. Feeling like this is still having the mindset of expecting to fail that you need to get out of. How long of watching memories would it take to treat a forty-year-old person to understand what they've been through and how they got here? Probably more than those forty years.

This is why I want you to walk alone without sounds, without technology, just the sound of your own thoughts, the sound of the world, the birds chirping, the dogs barking, the sound of kids playing, kids laughing, a gentle breeze cooling you off from the hot sun, out there on your own spiritually naked and open to the world.

"Time for you to come out the shadows, Junuh" (from *The Legend of Bagger Vance*). It's time for the person you were meant to be to rise out of the shadows that you have created to protect yourself from the world. Shadows created for a hateful world full of the disdain of its own failures and insecurities so much so that it drags everyone who lets it down to its level.

Be the joyful kid you were before the world told you that you shouldn't. Strip all of those layers you built up away. Expose it and forgive it. Forgive it deliberately. Say it out loud, write it down, type it out, whatever you need to do to bring it to light and just let it go. Just like a curling stone, you're sliding with the stone if you just let it go, you will begin to separate. You slow down and the rock keeps sliding getting farther and farther away. Soon, you can't even hear it sliding, it's just going off into the distance leaving you behind here still with the memories, but without the weight of the stone. (Thanks, Bill Burr! Kind of.)

If you want to tell someone else, that's fine, but it's your business because it's your mental health. If you feel sharing with someone else will help you expose it, that's great. I'm sure the comfort of another human to hug will help, as long as you let it go.

Every step is crucial because it leads to the next step, but this is the part that most people skip which is why they can lose weight but not keep it off. If you do not get rid of the root cause of a problem, it doesn't matter how many of the symptoms you cure, it will keep coming back. The mind drives the body, if you didn't get those bad thoughts out, they will continue to affect your behavior and your thinking.

This is still part of step number 1. Keep this going until you feel some kind of release, some kind of insight, some kind of moment of clarity. It will be different for everyone, but I know exactly when it happened for me, and you probably will too. If you need this book, it will probably not be subtle, which is why I said bring tissues or an extra towel.

JOURNEYING WITH ADDICTION

Most likely, needing this book, you are probably living with some kind of addiction. Healthy humans with a good chemical balance do not seek comfort food or alcohol or drugs if things are just fine, usually—there are exceptions, but we should all agree that that statement applies to 98 percent of people. I completely understand living with it, I sought out comfort from all of those things. Drinking, smoking, drugs, and food.

Ultimately, *Boil the Frog* is about making slow subtle changes to become the person you want to be, and anyone can do that. It's not just about weight loss, it's an overall attitude and mentality that even though a journey is one thousand miles, you can just take one step at a time and get there eventually. It's a personality that encompasses and acknowledges that life can be challenging, but it doesn't have to be an unbeatable opponent.

When walking through the past and finding root causes, acknowledging them, and forgiving them, these behaviors become apparent. You see why you seek out what you seek out when you are triggered. Get angry and it makes you want to smoke, so instead of smoking, you go for a walk until you calm down. During that process of getting your mind right, you are finding both the root cause and finding what triggers you, and you are altering your own behavior. Some people have such harsh root causes and triggers that they can't control themselves and binge whatever they are seeking in order to make themselves feel like they are whole, even for a few hours.

These are the people we call alcoholics, drug addicts, morbidly obese, sex addicts, etc. They feel like they can't control themselves because they have not figured out why they do it. I'm talking about every one of them. Even the ones who blatantly admit that they know what they are doing is killing them, because that is their goal. They want to die. They believe that the comfort they seek is more important than living without it. I can't tell you how wrong that is, but literally, if they were in their right mind, they never would think that way in the first place.

This will be a very unpopular opinion, but having done it both ways and seeing it both ways, I truly believe this. This applies to all the vices, but I know being and I know seeing an alcoholic, so that's what I will refer to. If you are an alcoholic, your body has become addicted to having that be part of its chemical make-up. You just feel "right" when you are on that chemical, until you overdo it that is. My opinion is that people have made themselves addicted to something and now the body depends on it, why on earth would you tell those people to stop taking it entirely?

I grew up with an alcoholic father that never took a drop of alcohol (not that I remembered) in my lifetime, and he was miserable. I overheard him once when somebody asked him if he still wanted to drink. His answer baffled me at the time: "Every day." Every day. To fight that urge every day for almost forty years, I would probably be miserable too, and I don't want that for my family.

Personally, I don't think an alcoholic has any business not drinking alcohol. I tried that too, and less is better than none and definitely better than too much. If you can tame that monster, you can live with it. Growing up seeing how an alcoholic without alcohol lives, I just don't see how he did it, especially if he wanted it every day. I suppose I know where I got my discipline from. I describe smoking the same way to people when they ask me, so I know it's forever. I want to smoke cigarettes every day still, and I haven't smoked for over six years. I kicked that without boiling the frog and that was not pleasant.

All those vices are something that your body literally craves, and their advice is to just stop doing it all together. Same as tackling a big project, you have to take it a little bit at a time. I am *not* talking about AA and their steps. I am talking about you sorting out your own mind and understanding why you are doing it. If you continuously search your mind, you will find the root cause, and you can acknowledge it and move on.

I don't, but medical professionals consider me an alcoholic because I drink at least three a day. So fine, I'm an alcoholic. But guess what? I figured out why during that process, and now I don't need ten to fourteen beers every day. As a matter of fact, I don't need one beer a day, but I enjoy them. So I drink two to four, depending on what I am doing and when I have to get up.

Point being, and back to the unpopular opinion, my body wants that alcohol on a daily basis. I have made it so with my behavior, and now I can just take enough for that craving to go away. It is possible to live with your own addiction. Just like this entire principle, you can live with it once you figure out the why of things and regulate how much you can have.

I don't care what it is, you can wean yourself down to a level where you are no longer dependent, and you can still enjoy it without over indulging. I know, I can already hear some of you: "Once I start, I just can't stop." That's popular with alcoholics. If you think that still, you still haven't got your mind right.

"Well, what about super addicting drugs, like crack?" Are you a crackhead or a smack head? I doubt people at that level of *screw it* will pick up this book, but I can't say for sure. I wouldn't know because I've never done super addictive drugs. You know why? *Because they are super addicting!* Regardless, if you are on crack reading this book, give it a try, wean back until you smoke your last. Nothing is impossible, always remember that.

Back to the opening paragraph when I said once you open yourself to the idea that you can accomplish anything you set your mind to, the infinite becomes possible. The total and complete belief in yourself and what you can do will conquer all doubts. The term *the infinite* is just a metric I use to measure the unmeasurable. To give value to something that could never possibly be counted given your entire lifetime. To really believe that you can do anything because nothing is too big to be conquered if you believe.

However big you believe your addiction is, your belief in yourself and your abilities to not only live with it, but to beat it, will triumph. It is not easy, just like everything else I am asking you to do, but it is possible, I have done it. I never ask or recommend anything to anyone else that I haven't already done myself. Nor should anyone else for that matter.

This is not theory I am preaching to you; this is a recollection of real life events that recently transpired for my life. It's an accomplishment. This is real life changes that will actually matter to you. That will actually change your life, your *whole* life, for the better. Having an addiction is just one more problem to overcome, and nothing is impossible.

That food, that drug, that drink, that smoke, all of those things cannot make you happy for the long term. That's something you need to understand on your own; it can't be taught, only learned. Look at whatever you are doing—or all of those things for some people—and just understand that the temporary feeling those things give you, just keep lowering your own emotional bar each time you seek them out with a trigger, so even when the feeling fades, you are less happy than before you did it once it wears off.

You will find that, eventually, you can live without them, or at least live with them at a reasonable level so you don't need it, you want it. Moreover, you will be able to regulate it because you are keeping track. You see how much you are doing and know it's too much.

I can tell this chapter will probably be butchered by people who don't understand, but those I reach on a personal level know exactly what I'm talking about, and it can be done. Yes, I am advocating that people who are addicted to something not stop it, but slowly phase it down over a period of time. It has to be their own time and their own idea, otherwise, it will not work.

People have to have that choice. They have to know that they are quitting something or cutting back on something because it's their idea. Forcing behaviors onto people just increases their need for whatever they are trying to get rid of. I was forced to quit things, and everything that was forced on me I picked back up eventually once it stopped being enforced.

I quit smoking for two months when I was in boot camp, but the first thing I bought after I got out was a pack of cigarettes. Eventually, many years later, I did use vaping to taper off my smoking until I was able to quit, and I have quit now for over six years.

I slowly phased out cigarettes and replaced it with vaping. I started alternating smoke breaks from real cigarettes one time to vaping the next time. What I began to notice is that I felt horrible (in comparison) after smoking a real cigarette. I could literally feel it in my chest, that it was irritating my lungs. So I stepped up the vaping more, I changed from every other, to two vapes for one cigarette.

My body slowly began to realize I didn't want the cigarette smoke because, frankly, it made me feel like crap after. That's just another way to show your body that it doesn't need that, it just wanted something that was part of that, and you can phase it out. Moreover, I kept changing the nicotine level on my vaping lower and lower until I began vaping 0 mg nicotine. I only lasted a week of doing that before my body realized I didn't need *that* either. Now I have a pack a day, sugar-free Trident addiction and clear lungs.

The exact same strategy I used when I cut back my drinking. I mixed in two non-alcoholic beers for every real beer until I got down to no more than three to four a day. Down from eight to fourteen, that's pretty impressive, if I do say so myself. I did keep it up until I quit drinking alcohol entirely, over the course of about a month, but that whole week, I couldn't sleep more than three to four hours. So I can go without it entirely, but I choose not to. I enjoy my beers now, I don't gulp them just to get drunk, and I can absolutely stop if I want to.

Granted, that is the go-to saying for people with a problem, I know, but that is actually true in my case, and it can be true in yours. Addiction is not impossible to overcome, but you have to understand why you have it and how to taper it off. Just like every other "impossible" obstacle you encounter, it can be overcome once you understand that you can. Which is what? Getting your mind right. Your mind can conquer all and more life has to throw at you.

It is the exact same way you can control overeating. Just slowly replace the bad things with good things and your body will like it. Then you will go to eat the bad thing, and your body will be, like, *nope*. Bang. Feel like crap again because you ate crap.

- Apples instead of chips
- Green beans instead of French Fries
- Wheat Bread for white bread
- Turkey instead of ham
- Boca Burgers instead of real ground beef

The combinations are infinite. There is always a different thing you can eat instead of the unhealthy option. Point being, you have choices to substitute to allow you to quit bad things all over the place. They might cost more, they might be harder to find, but we do not train to be easy here we train to be hard.

> *We do not train to be merciful here. Mercy is for the weak.*
> —John Kreese in *The Karate Kid*

COMFORT ZONES

Like some people here, I suffer from social anxiety. I get really uncomfortable when there is a lot of people around. I suppose it probably reminds me of high school. This is not a pleasant memory. Being bullied and made fun of any time I actually showed any effort throughout my scholastic times or if they just felt like humiliating an easy target. So always being the nerd or the dork or the geek, if you tried something, the popular kids made fun of you. That was just the way of the world back then, probably still and worse with social media nowadays. What's worse is that I was so devastated when it happened, it showed easily. That just made it worse. When someone does something that they can see affects you, they will just keep doing it as long as they get the reaction they are looking for.

I realize that now, looking back, walking back through the past, I understand it. I was already uncomfortable with whatever I was doing, and people made fun of me just to see me go over the edge. If I had simply just not reacted, if I had simply just been comfortable with the fact that the person making fun of me, was amidst the best four years of their life, smiled at them, and moved on, I would have had a much easier time in high school, and it wouldn't have affected me for years after the fact.

When I spoke to my mom about being bullied or made fun of, my mom told me, what I thought, at the time, was the dumbest possible way to respond to them. She told me when someone makes fun of you, just smile at them/give a little chuckle, and walk away. *That is so stupid*, I thought. How will that even come close to working? Little did I know how effective that would have been. When someone expects a reaction and you give them the exact opposite, they don't know what to do. It's a learned pattern, just like your reactions become.

Part of my layers was to protect against criticism, and it's harsh. That layer of my reacting harshly, as harsh as possible, was a direct learned behavior of shoving that feeling down and never reacting when I was younger. I was skinny and easy to push around, both mentally and physically, so standing up for myself at that time would be suicidal in my own mind. That's what I thought, and that's how I acted. The mind drives the body, just like I said.

However, the not-reacting caused inner anger, anger I never showed until some little thing or big thing sent me over the edge, and I exploded. Usually at inanimate objects. Even before I got my mind right, I knew that that wasn't healthy. But I wasn't comfortable doing it any other way.

"Be comfortable being uncomfortable." "Get out of your comfort zone." I'm sure you heard it all as I have. I told you that quick back story to give you the way forward if you are like me and just not comfortable socially and with other people. You have to understand that, yes, other people bullied you, but these are not those people.

Do yourself a favor, put down the defenses. Walking through the past should have shown you that you have developed this thick skin for reasons that are no longer relevant. People like me that developed the bullied layer to combat embarrassment or repressed anger, from peons that just wanted to feel powerful that day and you were an easy target.

When I looked at the past, the people that bothered me the most, I literally never saw them again after high school. They did not matter in my life after that part of my life was over. So why did I still have that layer? I don't need it! I developed a permanent solution to a temporary problem and did so for almost twenty years.

It is time you got out of your comfort zone and relearn what it is like to function normally. It is your fundamental duty as an adult to unlearn bad behaviors and learn good ones. You are not "permanently" messed up, you just need to change it the same way others changes it for you. You don't have to be on guard all of the time. That time is over; those people are gone. If you have "friends" that make fun of you the same way, fire their ass. You don't have to tolerate being treated less than you feel you are. You can speak up without fear, you can say what you think because you *are* important.

Finding and expanding your comfort zone only empowers yourself. Those bullies in school had so much power over me because they just kept making my comfort zone smaller and smaller each day, breaking me down. I held that anger in, and it was not healthy at all.

Your comfort zone needs to be challenged. You should do at least one thing a week you either have no desire to do or think you shouldn't do (keep it legal). Timothy Ferris in *The 4-Hour Work Week* challenged all readers to comfort challenges. "Ask for the attractive person's phone number," or "Spontaneously lay down on the floor for ten seconds and don't move." Things like that, just do something.

If you are not exactly Mr. or Mrs. Personality, randomly compliment someone each day. Be genuine about and sincere. If you really are a monster like I used to be, you can get some weird looks, so just make sure they understand that you mean it and are not making fun of them.

This all goes back to challenging your mind, and you can even make a game out of it if you have close enough friends. You can do comfort texts where you tell them to do a random thing and they have to do it no matter where they are or who they are with. My favorite idea that I heard about is simply to text: "Shatner!" and wherever they are whoever they are talking to, they have to do it impersonating William Shatner as he acted in *Star Trek*. (The rumor is that his agent told him to use pauses in his lines so it would increase his camera time so that's how he developed that staggered, slow, speech pattern that we all know from that show.)

Can you imagine having that experience with someone? Just talking normally to someone, they get a text, and all of a sudden the person just starts into full character mode of William Shatner? That would be as confusing as it was hilarious.

This is *all* part of getting you to believe in yourself. Expanding your comfort zone expands the notion that you *can* do anything. It reinforces the notion that you are unstoppable and can do anything. You can *Boil the Frog* on this, just like you can everything else, but do this. Start with once a week and just keep scaling it up, using compliments at first is a good appetizer to get you going. Soon enough, that will lead you to having conversations with complete strangers and becoming the very Mr./Mrs. Personality that you thought you weren't.

Even better is when you actually confront the people who think you are a pushover—those are people to use your comfort zone exercises on as well. Tell them what you think about how they treat you. It's unbelievably liberating to see their smug expression turn confused, and then angry because they understand they can't get your power anymore, you took it back.

Never forget that either: you have that power. That power is something you begin every day with and it's whatever you want it to be, and you use it however you want to. Don't let someone's twenty seconds ruin your twenty-four-hour day. Screw them, walk away. That's your power, you choose who gets it. No one else.

Standing up for yourself is definitely out of some people's comfort zones. I know that for a fact, I've seen it and I feel for them. These are even more important than the positive comfort zone exercises of complimenting and trying new things. This will help expand your zone faster than anything else when you tell a person who has talked down on you for years what you really think. That is huge for personal growth.

Just like everything else I'm asking, don't skip this. It all works together, and you just keep building on it and building on it, and eventually you have the mind and personality that you always wanted. You just have to understand that it is possible.

10,000 REASONS TO GET OUT OF BED IN THE MORNING

With all the preparation of the mind—understanding your past, walking through your past, forgiving your past, all of these things we do to get the mind right—like the social media meme says, "You can pray all day leaning against a shovel, but eventually you have to actually dig the hole yourself." All these tactics are setting you up for success, and here's where you really start chopping away at the pounds you want to shed.

This is the part where you downshift after the curve and accelerate. Once my mind was in a good place, I started setting step goals. I started with the standard I was told about by my friend Jeremy of 10,000 steps every day. This is designed so you lose one to one and a half pounds per week if you just add this to your routine all by itself. That is a good pace; any faster than this, and you might start to get dizzy and feel the need to binge eat.

Before you up your step count, let me add that as you increase your step count, your feet will begin to hurt. I highly recommend you get a good pair of metatarsal shoe inserts. I have several sets of the same kind for multiple footwear by a brand I got on Amazon called Dr. Foot's Arch Support Insoles. They are designed to help against plantar fasciitis, metatarsal and heel pain. No, I do not sell them. Yes, they are designed to combat lots of impacts throughout the day, say, ten thousand to twenty-five thousand little impacts.

All I know is that I was increasing my step count, and all of the sudden, my left metatarsal hurt all of the time. The relief when I put those insoles in was almost instantaneous, and after a few weeks I didn't have any more pain, so I highly recommend you find comfortable insoles that work for you. That took me a few tries with trying a couple other types and brands, but those worked best for me. Up until this point, my walks were not far enough to make my feet hurt, but that was about to change, so if you're ready beforehand, learn from my experience and save yourself some pain.

Now I was upping my game, ten thousand steps, which equates to about five miles depending on your stride length, but it averages to be about two thousand steps per mile for most people. That was my first real goal to get going. I wasn't even tracking calories yet; I was just getting my body used to changing from a sedentary lifestyle to an active lifestyle.

There have been studies that have shown that not all people can just lose weight walking ten thousand steps, and I'm not surprised. It's a culmination of combining tactics that work involving mental, physical, and dietary changes over your whole life. So, sure, you can look up ten thousand steps and see these posted studies show not everyone can lose weight doing just the steps and use it as an excuse not to do it if you want, but like I said, don't use someone else's failure to justify your own. You're better than that now, and you know it. You have already succeed where others have failed.

At this point, since you already got your mind right, if you want to include a walking buddy or music or talking feel free. Anything that gets you down the road and back again to reach your goal. I purchased some earbuds and was amazed how much farther I wanted to walk now that I had my own soundtrack. I was knocking out ten thousand steps a day no problem after that.

I work in a warehouse in my day job, and it's fairly large, so getting ten thousand steps in was not difficult at all for me. Some others may have time and space constraints, but that is okay. Initially, I was going for ten thousand steps per day, which included my job steps.

After a few weeks of this (and I sorted out my foot pain), I changed my goals to walk ten thousand steps, but they had to be all at the same time. Meaning, regardless of how many steps I got throughout the day, if I went for a walk, it had to be far enough to get those steps all at the same time. I think that is the real secret when it comes to steps accounting for weight loss.

I found a route that is 4.77 miles long. It is a route I still use today, only now I use it for running, but that is for talking about later. This route gave me the exact goal steps every day that I could do after work and still be home for dinner with the family. It took about one and half to two hours to walk that far (depending on your shape), so time to start downloading audio books.

Is that time consuming? Yes, of course. If it were easy, everyone would do it. You can stick with music, which I do often, or you can take this time for yourself to learn about everything you wanted to learn about. Want to learn a foreign language? How about practicing one to two hours every day? I downloaded business books, marketing books, how to analyze people, how to win friends and influence people, how to be a better husband and father, motivation books. Whatever you want, it's your journey. Most say they don't have the time; well, now you can combine efforts and double dip exercise and education at the same time. Just pay attention to the road!

If you are married, with a family, they will understand. They will start to see the changes in you, but discuss it with them just to be sure and explain what you are doing, and they should support you. They will start to see the physical changes, sure, but they will notice you are happier, have your emotions in better control, and will just sense your overall presence is different. I've had several friends look at me kind of sideways and say, "There's just something different about you, I can't put my finger on it."

I usually say, "Yup, it's called getting your act together."

With this slight change in my step goal, taking ten thousand all at once, I noticed a difference almost immediately. It also increased my step count to almost twenty-thousand per day as I was still getting in steps during work hours. Even trapped in that hotel room when I was quarantined, I got my ten thousand steps, twelve steps each lap at a time, walking back and forth. Even getting out of my chair was easier, my leg strength was increasing, and I was shedding pounds.

How many pounds? I wasn't sure, my digital scale had become somewhat unreliable due to age. It was then that I decided to start getting technology involved. I opted to purchase a Wyze smart scale and a Fitbit. That's when things became crystal clear and how I took things to the next level.

USING TECHNOLOGY TO OPTIMIZE YOUR GOALS

Up until this point, I was making small strides, I could see my weight slowly creeping down even just a month and a half into it. I had just began tracking calories on the Fitbit app, but until my actual Fitbit arrived, it was showing a generic burn rate for calories based on height, weight, and age. I knew I was burning more than that and really wanted it to arrive so I could really start targeting my burn calorie and intake calorie goals, all of which you can set up on the app.

My Fitbit arrived on June 18, 2021, and in working with the app, it recommended getting a smart scale. I didn't right away, but I realized it was right, and I eventually I purchased a Wyze smart scale about a month later so I could start tracking my body fat percentage and other things like muscle mass, etc. You can also set up an app for your smart scale, and it will share data with the Fitbit app, working in tandem.

Previously I mentioned that I couldn't believe how many calories I was consuming once I started logging every calorie every day, and this is the time period that really opened my eyes. I said you can eat fast food and still lose weight, but at this time, I had no idea what those calories numbers on the menu actually meant until I started actually tracking them. Once I did? Holy crap.

I was eating 1,000 1,500 calorie lunches just going out to lunch with the guys from work every day. My wife is also a phenomenal cook and even dinners were pushing 1,000 calories. Top that off with me finishing the evening in my chair, watching TV with another high-calorie snack and beer on top of it. I was putting away almost

3,500 to 4,000 calories per day! I can't even believe I lost weight at all in the beginning!

Now that my head was out of the sand, the other ostriches looked ridiculous. I knew I needed portion control at the very minimum, and diet change if possible. As I already wrote, I wasn't quite ready to give up on the foods that I loved, but I did decide that I could change how much of everything I had. So that's what I did.

The medium Italian sub on Italian bread I used to eat with chips and a drink? I skipped the chips, change the bread to whole wheat, and I would eat half of the sandwich and save the other have as a snack later or eat it again for lunch the next day. I still have my soda, but my new philosophy with soda is that it's fine to enjoy with a meal, but once you are done, put it away or throw it away. No more than the equivalent of one total twelve-ounce can per day either.

My wife's dinners were still awesome, but I would not fill up my plate entirely and would really try not to get seconds (sometimes her unbelievable mac and cheese just called me back). I would look up what we were eating before it was ready, and measure out how much there is (like a cup or six ounces) and log it. I figured I would have to start averaging about 500 calories per meal to meet my intake calorie goal of 2,000 to 2,500 each day.

That allowed me a little room in the evening for a snack, and I could still drink a little beer. I also began throwing in non-alcoholic beer in the mix to save calories that way as well. Two fake beers, then two real beers. This saved calories immediately and got me even closer to my goal. I know. I can hear you screaming at the book, "Just quit it entirely!" Like I said, boil the frog. Slowly phasing things in and out is the secret to success. Just like I wasn't yet willing to give up on my favorite foods, I wasn't ready to give up my beer just then.

Speaking of giving things up, don't cheat. Use these apps and technology to your advantage as they should be so you need to log every calorie and every ounce of water you are consuming—every day, please. The only drawback from the Fitbit app, is that you have to manually enter all you are consuming. If you forget, it literally has no idea. So best practice is to log things before you eat them making sure you are logging every calorie every day.

If you are burning more than you are taking in, you should not be gaining weight. I can literally already hear people saying that they did everything I said, and they still gained weight. If you are, you are not logging everything. Sorry, but it's not possible. Your calorie burn rate should be at least 25 to 30 percent higher than your intake. For 2,500 calories of intake, that equates to a 3250 burn rate, every day. Just multiply your intake by 1.3 and that's what you should be burning every day, until you meet your goal. You should also be consuming sixty-four ounces of water every day.

Another great thing about the Fitbit app (I promise I don't work for them or get compensated in anyway. Again, just telling you exactly what I did), you can literally scan the barcodes on the food packages, and it will log every calorie, carb, fat, vitamins, etc. So you can not only get the convenience of logging your meals with just a picture scan, if it's in the Fitbit system, it already has all the ingredients loaded so you can see your micronutrient counts each day. (If it's not in the system, you can request it be entered by giving a minute or two of information to them, and they will eventually add it.) How many carbs you ate, how much grams of fat and protein you consumed, it documents it all so you can plainly see how much of everything you are taking in. Once you start to see that, you're like, "No wonder I was packing on the pounds!"

Using the app, I could track things so well that I could gradually cut back little things every day here and there to reduce my calorie intake. I would start to think, *Do I really need this, or do I just want this?* I got rid of the after-dinner treat. I used to have a Halloween bowl of candy that was filled year-round, and I would eat one to two (usually two, let's be honest) of those mini candy bars after dinner every night. Did I need that? Nope. Cut it out. Those little candy bars (Put it down! I see you!) were just adding 100 to 140 calories to my intake.

Did I give it up forever? Of course not, but I didn't need them right then, so I cut those out because it was hurting my chances of fulfilling my goals. I do sometimes indulge in deserts on special occasions—as you should; don't forget to actually enjoy life. Eating birthday cake and ice cream, enjoying desert on your anniversary.

They are treats! You should eat them rarely and keep them special; they are not for daily consumption. Just account for the occasional extra calories by adding to your burn rate for the day.

I finally kept it going and cut out enough calories until I got to the point that I was continuously averaging about 2,500 calories per day. The goal was to get down to 2,000 to 2,100, but considering I used to eat that much in just two meals, I was taking the small victory. Little by little is how you can do it. Skip something here and there, and eventually, you will reach your goal. That goal should be the same as mine about 2,000 to 2,500.

Now that I knew how many calories I was consuming and made the necessary changes to get those calories down to a reasonable level, I started watching how many calories I was actually burning, which the Fitbit does an excellent job of tracking. I could literally see what I needed to do on a screen right in front of me.

The goal was simple in premise, but harder (not impossible) to put in the action. At that time, I was down to about 220 pounds. I had lost around fifteen pounds in the first two months just walking and not changing my calories. My body was starting to adapt, and the pounds were going away at a slower rate, so I knew I needed not just to lower my calorie intake but to step it up and burn 1,500 calories more than I was consuming. I set my calorie burn rate to 4,000 calories per day and tried to stay under 2,500 calories per day.

Well, what about the scale? I almost forgot. The great thing about the smart scale is it calculates your body fat percentage (among other things), so it gives you a new metric to see and a new goal to set. You have to stand on it barefoot and what it does is it works with the help of sensors underneath your feet. According to a Google search, "when you step on the scale, a small electrical current runs up through your leg and across your pelvis, measuring the amount of resistance from body fat."

When I started on the scale, I was over 20 percent body fat but didn't really know what that meant so I looked that up too. Depending on what chart you use in your search, it may be a little different, but for the sake of moving things forward, I used one I found online and for my age group and gender, 20 percent is considered overfat, 15 to 19 percent is considered healthy, and 10 to 14 percent is ideal. Less than 10 percent is considered underfat, and is usually where the body builders and models tend to live. I'm sure they are hungry. Regardless, you should look up your own specifics based on your age and gender so you will have another goal to set.

Speaking of goals, part of my sedentary lifestyle was playing video games. I used to be able to sit in my chair for hours at a time (not anymore, but used to). One of my favorite kind of games were role-playing games (RPG) like Final Fantasy or the Sims, and I would just level those guys up. For hours, I would roam the game's map just level up those characters. What I realized was that with the app, I was playing a real-life RPG and just watching my stats increase.

In this instance, I was watching my stats go down. My weight was going down, my resting heart rate was going down, my calorie intake was down, etc. I had realized that life is exactly like an RPG, and I had been focusing on the wrong stats. Now that I could see those stats electronically displayed for me, I treated it the same as an RPG. I could do the real-life mundane tasks we put off because they don't seem important in a single sitting, but when you put all those things together you realize you really do have something.

If I was willing to do the mundane tasks to get to where I needed to be in a video game that literally meant nothing to me in a real-world practical application, why couldn't I max out my real-life stats? I decided I could, and I could do almost all of it just through calorie awareness. That's how the technology took me to the next level.

I wasn't just out there walking, I had data I could actually look at and see how it was transforming me! It was really great to see every graph on the app that I wanted to go down and every category I wanted to see go up do exactly that. I was crushing it, and I could see it! Even though my body wasn't quite starting to look like it, my body on the inside was changing according to the app. Those are results, and results will keep people motivated.

So many people quit at first because they don't "see" results right away; however, when you start tracking things on apps, it is literally right in front of you to see that you are making changes in your body even if they haven't translated to your physical appearance yet. As I said before, it took you a long time to have the body that makes you want to change your life. It will not happen overnight, but I know you *all* are on your phones all of the time, just like everyone else. Might as well use its powers for good.

I know I was considered obese by BMI standards, but I wasn't as overweight as other people that are going to start their journey with this book. I just want you to be aware of exactly how long it took me. From the time I started walking on May 1 until I reached my "ideal weight" goal was five months and three days. From 235 pounds to 175 pounds, 60 pounds in five months and three days just from calorie awareness, portion control, and calorie burn goals achieved daily. In other words, the dreaded phrase: Diet and Exercise.

This was achieved by calories and just walking and running to accomplish my step goals. Nothing more. I fully understand I started in a way better place than a lot of people, and I know that it will take people like that even longer, but the length of the journey really doesn't matter. Six months from now doesn't matter for your goals. Today is the only day you can count today, and these technologies that are available make it so much easier to see your progress and keep your motivation at a high level.

You can only boil that frog to beat who you were yesterday and make strides each day to improve. Remember the bamboo tree story. You have to keep watering your dreams every day, and eventually you can see those dreams realized. It could be months from now it could be years from now. You only have to do your best today and just keep moving forward. You have unbelievable power inside of you, and you can call on it anytime you want.

You can slow down toward achieving your goals but don't ever stop moving forward. People have waved at me and pointed at my shoe. I knew what they are pointing at—my shoelace which became untied about two miles back (sometimes both of them, but I have runner's laces now so that doesn't happen). I only respond with, "Can't stop. Won't stop!" I can't let a small thing like an untied shoe stop me from beating my yesterday, can I? Heck no. As long as my shoe is still on my foot, it doesn't matter. Those little things that want to stop you do not matter. They are just excuses; ignore them and keep going. Unless it's cops, then yeah, stop. Barring police involvement, keep moving forward.

Once you get into the technology, you really start to see what is working, and then you really start to be goal-oriented. That's what you need to start asking yourself: What is your real goal? Where do you want to get to? You cannot water a seed if it's not in the ground. Figure it out and set it in your mind what that goal is to have something to strive for. I didn't really know what I wanted in the beginning other than to feel and look better, and that's okay to get you moving, but if you really want to zero in your focus, you need to have an actual achievable goal to shoot for. A target to focus on.

With these apps, I was able to see where I wanted to get to and get there. Once you achieve your goal, set another one just as big as the first. When I achieved my weight loss number goal, I immediately set another goal to take this fat loss and turn it into muscle. Not just muscle, six-pack abs level fat loss and muscle sculpting to keep my behavior going with the calorie awareness but use that to get down to 10 percent body fat or less and continually transform my body into a statuesque shape.

Just try not to go lower than 8 percent; that's considered under-fat, and it's kind of like holding your breath. You can do it for a while, but don't stay down there too long; it's not healthy. Those body builders and models diet and exercise to be in peak shape for a competition or a photoshoot and then they *usually* drift back up to a more manageable body fat percentage. Some of them get down to 1 to 3 percent body fat for a competition. That. Is. Crazy.

HEALTHY HABITS

In case you didn't know it yet, you're going to have to make some changes in your life if you really want to lose the weight and become healthy. I prefer to use the term *healthy habits* rather than *diet*. Diet just throws up a red flag for people that means "restricting yourself."

That is really not the case because you are not restricting anything; you are changing your habits to eat better food or just plain less of the bad food. Change is just as scary a word as restricted to some people, I get it. I am an obsessive-compulsive disorder (OCD) case study over here, so I get that change is hard, so if I can manage, anyone can.

Here's what you need to understand and literally talk yourself into: the changes you are making for a healthier lifestyle will carry over to every facet of your life. Moreover, once the changes start happening, you will be so thrilled with the results you will tell yourself it wasn't really that hard (action removes fear). Your mind starts formulating an opinion to the positive side once the results start actually working, i.e., losing pounds, body shape is looking better, it's easier to get up out of a chair, or just feel better overall.

I was a straight-up carnivore up until a few years ago—very rarely ate vegetables, never ate salads, and always requested "no lettuce and no tomato" on anything that came with it, and no pickles. I really don't even remember why, but one day I bought some V8 Healthy Greens. No one was more shocked than me.

I brought it home and as soon as I poured a glass of it and looked at it, I thought: *I just wasted my money again.* I'm going to take one sip and throw this away. It looked hideous. It was a straight-up green juice that looked like you would spit it out as far as you possibly could once it hit your taste buds. I looked at the ingredients, and here are the ingredients listed in order or abundance in the actual juice:

- Sweet Potatoes
- Yellow Carrots
- Cucumber
- Celery
- Kale
- Romaine lettuce
- Green Pepper
- Spinach
- Apples
- Pineapple

I direct you to look at all these ingredients and try and figure out what this concoction would taste like. I kind of shook my head closed my eyes and took a sip. Sweet mother of pearls…that…is…delicious! In one of those dramatic turn of events, the final ingredient on the list, the last item on the list, is so potent that it dominates the flavor.

All those greens and healthy items were smuggled inside my body under the guise of pineapple juice. That's all I could taste. My body was finally getting what I had been depriving it of for all those years, and it wanted more. After the first test sip, I drank it all at once.

After that, slowly but surely (boil the frog), I was adding more vegetables and greens into my diet and my body aches that I didn't really notice before were going away. The rib cramps, the irritated gallbladder started fading, the fatty liver pains went away, all of the things I was just used to living with were suddenly fading away. Eating a "balanced" diet was now starting to make me feel better. I would keep the lettuce and tomato and onions on my subs and enjoyed them.

I could stomach eating salads now, though I still don't really eat them that much. I feel like I need to add so much to it to combat the lack of flavor that I'm countering the effects of eating a salad. I make them at home for a short while, but mostly I eat them when they come with a meal eating out at a restaurant now instead of declining it and share it with my wife.

Point to all of that is that I made one subtle change by starting to drink the V8 healthy greens juice, and my body thanked me for it. I phased all of that in over a long period, and now I was actually eating a balanced diet. I'm still primarily a carnivore, but I look for some veggies to go with it, so I'm officially an omnivore now.

Here's the kicker. If you revert and go back to unhealthy eating habits, your body is now spoiled and will react like a toddler whose favorite toy just got taken away. Those pains you blocked out before, they come back, only now, you really notice that they are there now. When something is unpleasant for long enough, your mind just has to stop reacting to it or it would use all of its energy sounding the alarm. Eventually, it figures out you either don't care or, like most, are just not going to do anything about it and turn it off.

All of a sudden your body really is a temple and when the bandits come in, your body reacts harshly to this newly christened holy ground. Now that is has had the good stuff, that's what it wants. All of a sudden instead of chips as a snack, you're eating granola bars. Instead of a cupcake, you're eating a banana or fruit cups as a dessert. Point is your body knows what it needs to succeed and perform at optimum levels. When you are stepping up your exercises, this is when it craves those things to replenish what you have used.

So yes, you can eat what you want, unless otherwise directed by a doctor, but you're going to realize that the foods that used to be your favorite are really not good for your body, and your body recognizes that now that it has seen a better way to operate your body at peak function.

I used to love cheeseburgers (Five Guys was my temple), but now I rarely eat a real one because they make me have indigestion, and I just don't feel good after that. The rib muscle pains come back, the pressure around your heart (that was there all of the time before and you just didn't notice) comes back. You just don't feel good. It may have tasted delicious, but now your body is spoiled. It has had

93-octane premium gas and when you try and put regular 87-octane unleaded, it doesn't like it. Because that is exactly what food is: fuel.

I use premium in my cars to make them run better. I never correlated healthy food being fuel until I stepped up to it and then stepped back. You really feel the difference in the performance, much like once you switch in your car you feel the performance change as well. It used to be subtle, but now it is very obvious.

There are plenty of healthy foods that still taste good, and there are plenty of bad foods that taste phenomenal. These delicious foods like candy bars, cakes, and desserts are the types that *are* about tasting good. They are a treat. You are either celebrating a special occasion or rewarding yourself for your hard work. You don't have to cut them out entirely, just use it how it was intended—as a treat. They are *not* for daily consumption; otherwise, they are just bad food part of a bad diet, and they lose the specialness of being a treat. The rarity of these treats are what is supposed to make them so special.

I still eat them on occasion, but I savor them more now because of their rarity. I used to wolf these down in a couple of bites, but now I take very tiny bites and eat it very slowly, enjoying every moment that it is moving over my taste buds. Much as the difference in how I drink beer. I sip it now and enjoy it, and never more than three in a day unless it's a Saturday and I splurge to four.

This is the exact same philosophy I use when I do have fast food on occasion. Fast food is not out entirely if you want; however, if you plan on making it under your calorie goals on a daily basis (and you should, that's the only way this works), then those calorie-packed items are going to make that difficult. Eating out is the same as desserts, a treat that should be rare. No more than once or twice in a month is ideal.

Healthy habits are just as much of a discipline as exercising regularly. You always have to remember that you are boiling the frog slowly where it will not jump out. You are doing this slowly over time, phasing in things that are good and phasing out things that are bad. You are reading this book in a few hours, days, or weeks, but this took months to do all of these things. As Emperor Hadrian told his Romans, "Brick by brick, my citizens. Brick by brick."

The emperor's quote is a reflection of this slow, careful, methodical, and responsible building of healthy habits that are sustainable and will prevent or severely dissuade regression back to unhealthy habits. This is what you are doing with your body. Giving it the right materials over the right amount of time, and your body will not only be onboard, but it will also thank you with feeling great, looking great, and performing when you ask it to.

Everything we are doing is over a long period of time so you and your body can adapt to it. It will be worth the wait, trust me. Remember, this is a real-life RPG, it takes a lot of time to get your ratings up, so don't rush it. You are in this for the long haul, building a solid foundation.

If you were like me, you can experiment. Of course, not everyone is going to like the same things. There are people that flat-out take bites of five-inch pickles right in front of me, and it makes me want to gag. There is a reason I am not telling you exactly what to eat because you have to find what works for you. What you can stomach, what you can live without, what you can substitute. No one else is doing this for you; this is work, this is effort. This is not *just* a diet; it is a total and complete lifestyle change—from the mind to the belly.

The more you do, the more you change toward healthy habits, the better the results will be. If the results don't happen, then put in more effort! Moreover, let the results take the time to work, if you give up in a week or two because it's hard, then those are the results you are going to get—nothing. If you give this a true effort, which is a minimum of ninety days to start seeing real life-changing effects, you will not fail, I promise you that.

MAINTAIN

Here is the area some people have trouble with: maintaining what they lost. If you are there, that's awesome, I'm so proud of you. But you have to transition your mentality just the same as you did when you went into weight-loss mode. You need to prepare your mind for changing up tactics.

Imagine you are sliding down a hill and you are coming to the end of the run, what do you do? You should put your feet on the ground and slowdown of course. Same goes with getting out of weight-loss mode and going into maintaining healthy weight mode.

Now you don't have to cut as many calories as you did before and don't have to burn as much. You may even feel guilty about having a few extra calories. It's normal after months of fighting that having peace feels weird. You just have to remember at this point that you made it! You don't have to fight and struggle anymore, you are here, you are at your goal! Now it is really time to coast, time for the slow victory lap in life.

When I was in full weight-loss mode, I had a daily calorie burn goal of 4,000 and a calorie intake goal of 2,000 to 2,500 for five months. I maintained that, but sometimes I exceeded my intake limits, like on nights we were having fun or celebrating, or just special occasions that you should not have your diet participate in. You just have to make sure, as I did, that if you are going to exceed your intake limits for the day that you put in the work beforehand, so it doesn't matter because I certainly never burned less than I took in, even on those days.

The best way to get out of that mode is to deliberately intake more than you burn in one day. It is a good feeling to look on my Fitbit app and see the "red" bar graph showing I ate more calories

109

than I burned that day and know it doesn't matter, because I'm in maintenance mode.

I met my goal; now I'm just keeping it there, which means a mix of in-zone and some out-of-zone days. In-zone days are days that you are just about even with calorie intake and calories burned. On the Fitbit, it's represented by a green bar. Out-of-zone is represented by a red bar, meaning your intake exceeded your calories burned that day.

I still do my workouts most days, but they are about building muscle now, not about losing weight. Making sure you're eating proteins to build muscle and maintain a healthy weight. There is a wealth of information during this time in our history. You can literally learn most everything from instructional videos you can find online.

I constantly search for ideas for new workouts to target specific muscle groups. That's just me, though. If you are happy with just losing the weight, that is great! Just watch your intake and burn rate and keep up with exercise about three days a week. That's all you really need to do to maintain now that you are at your goal weight.

For those who went seven days a week like I did, this can be a challenge. But now that you are at your goal weight, it's time to start enjoying life. You don't have to go seven days a week; you just have to maintain, if that's what you want. If you want to amp it up and go for a six-pack like I'm doing, then you just change your methods and focus instead. However, unlike walking, when you are muscle building, you absolutely need to take rest days.

You don't have to go for weight training. This is just for those that want more now that they have it to show off. But the same principle still applies, whatever you do, just adapt to it slowly. Boil that frog.

MY CALORIE INTAKE EXAMPLES

While it is up to you to find your healthy habit niche, it is up to me to describe exactly what I did so you can have a road map on how to get there. You may take different roads, but the destination is the same. I have pulled up a few days as examples from my Fitbit logs.

Some from my highest calorie days and some from my lowest calorie days. I will put the dates on them so you can see how it transitions over time and you can see how those big calorie items can wreck your calorie count for the entire day.

- Sunday, June 13 (First Fitbit log day): 2807 calories
  - o Breakfast: 307 calories
    - Egg, sausage, healthy greens juice, coffee, coffee creamer.
  - o Lunch: 585 calories
    - Jalapeno-and-cheddar smoked sausage, hot dog buns, ketchup, light mayonnaise, diced jalapeno peppers, nacho taco blend cheddar cheese, banana.
  - o Afternoon Snack: 350 calories
    - Peanut Butter and Jelly Sandwich
  - o Dinner: 773 calories
    - Buffalo chicken wings, mac-and-cheese with Velveeta, Coca-Cola.
  - o Evening Snack: 792 calories
    - Budweiser Zero, Miller Lite, pepperoni pizza, Frosted Flakes cereal bar.

111

- o Macronutrients
  - ▪ 46% Carbs (277 g)
  - ▪ 38% Fat (117 g)
  - ▪ 16% Protein (108 g)

- Saturday, June 26 (largest calorie day of my logs): 4230 calories
  - o Breakfast: 350 calories
    - ▪ Egg, bacon, wheat bread, V8 Healthy Greens
  - o Lunch: 610 calories
    - ▪ McDouble, small fries.
  - o Dinner: 483 calories
    - ▪ BBQ Ribs, sweet peas
  - o Evening Snack: 2787 calories
    - ▪ Stuffed Crust Pizza, Miller Lite (14), Budweiser Zero (6)
  - o Macronutrients
    - ▪ 56% Carbs (314 g)
    - ▪ 28% fat (123 g)
    - ▪ 16% protein (119 g)

- Wednesday, July 21: 1903 calories
  - o Breakfast: 334 Calories
    - ▪ Egg, sausage patty, whole wheat toast, coffee and creamer, V8 Healthy greens
  - o Lunch: 384 Calories
    - ▪ Chicken parmesan, Coca-Cola
  - o Dinner: 584 calories
    - ▪ Mexican-style casserole, white rice, Coca-Cola
  - o Evening Snack: 601 calories
    - ▪ Budweiser Zero (4), Miller Lite (3)
  - o Macronutrients
    - ▪ 63% Carbs (242 g)
    - ▪ 19% Fat (39 g)
    - ▪ 18% Protein (73 g)

- Wednesday, August 18: 1965 calories
  - o Breakfast: 256 calories
    - Eggs (2), coffee and creamer, V8 Healthy Greens
  - o Morning Snack: 90 calories
    - Banana
  - o Lunch: 320 calories
    - Pepper steak meal
  - o Afternoon Snack: 100 calories
    - Chewy Chocolate Chip Granola Bar
  - o Dinner: 453 calories
    - Fried chicken leg, French-style green beans, baby carrots, Coca-Cola, Reese's Peanut Butter Cup.
  - o Evening Snack: 746 calories
    - Turkey with cheddar sausage, whole wheat bread, ketchup, Budweiser Zero (4), Miller Lite (3), chocolate chip cookie.
  - o Macronutrients
    - 58% Carbs (238 g)
    - 27% Fat (60 g)
    - 15% Protein (62 g)

- Wednesday, September 8: 1736 calories
  - o Breakfast: 326 calories
    - Egg (2), whole wheat toast, V8 Healthy greens, coffee and creamer
  - o Morning Snack: 90 calories
    - Banana
  - o Lunch: 360 calories
    - Chicken-fried beef steak meal
  - o Afternoon Snack: 260 calories
    - Protein shake, Chewy Granola Bar S'mores
  - o Dinner: 262 calories
    - BBQ ribs, French-cut green beans
  - o Evening Snack: 438 calories
    - Miller Lite (3), Budweiser Zero (3)
  - o Macronutrients

- ▪ 52% Carbs (178 g)
- ▪ 28% Fat (54 g)
- ▪ 20% Protein (76 g)

- Wednesday, October 13: 2133 calories
  - o Breakfast: 379 calories
    - ▪ Egg, whole wheat toast, sausage patty, V8 Healthy Greens, coffee and creamer,
  - o Morning Snack: 90 calories
    - ▪ Banana
  - o Lunch: 415 calories
    - ▪ Sweet-and-sour chicken, Coca-Cola
  - o Afternoon Snack: 270 calories
    - ▪ Protein Shake, Chewy Chocolate Chip Granola Bar.
  - o Dinner: 579 calories
    - ▪ Sweet-and-sour chicken, pork lo mein, white rice, Hunan stir-fry beef
  - o Evening Snack: 400 calories
    - ▪ Modelo (2), Budweiser Zero (2)
  - o Macronutrients
    - ▪ 62% Carbs (285 g)
    - ▪ 23% Fat (54 g)
    - ▪ 15% Protein (78 g)

- Wednesday, October 27 (yesterday at this time): 1880 calories
  - o Breakfast: 322 calories
    - ▪ Toasted oat cereal, whole milk, coffee and creamer
  - o Morning Snack: 95 calories
    - ▪ Oats n' Honey Granola Bar
  - o Lunch: 332 calories
    - ▪ Herb-roasted chicken, Coca-Cola, Oats n' Honey Granola Bar
  - o Afternoon Snack: 22 calories
    - ▪ Coffee and creamer
  - o Dinner: 435 calories

- Lumpia, protein shake and green juice blend, Dr. Pepper.
  - Evening Snack: 674 calories
    - Mexican-style casserole, Fat-free cottage cheese, Nacho Taco blend cheddar, Sun Maid raisins.
  - Macronutrients
    - 51% Carbs (244 g)
    - 25% Fat (53 g)
    - 24% Protein (111 g)

That may all be in Greek to you right now, but once you start tracking your calories, come back to this list and review it. You will see distinctive but subtle changes made over time. Slowly shifting from mostly carbs to adding more protein, adding better foods, calorie counts are getting consistent, I eat more snacks to get through to the next meal. The most important thing missing on the last list is the lack of beer in the evening snack.

The beauty of all of this is that out of all of those days listed above, if you check the logs on my Fitbit, only one of them was a positive calorie day. Meaning I ate more calories than I burned, which day do you think it was? The first one, and that's only because I didn't have my actual Fitbit yet, and it was using generic average burn rates based on my height and weight and didn't account for any exercise that day.

If that was accurately tracking my burn rate, I'm sure that would be a negative calorie day as well. This is why I am urging you not to just guesstimate things, but to get technology involved. You can do it either way, but given the choice between knowing and guessing, I will take knowing every time. With the exception of that first day which it wasn't tracking yet, let's look at the burn rates for those days as well.

Date	Calories In	Calories Out	Net Calories
June 13, 2021	2807	1966	+851
June 26, 2021	4230	5335	-1105

July 21, 2021	1903	4616	-2713
August 18, 2021	1965	3944	-1979
September 8, 2021	1736	3976	-2240
October 13, 2021	2133	3602	-1469
October 27, 2021	1880	4011	-2131

Most of these example days are my running days, with the exception of June 26—that was a Saturday and the day I take care of my yardwork that takes several hours, and it's a hang out with friends' night, so the company makes the beer plentiful (it used to anyway). I run 4.75 to 5 miles during those big burn days, and I'm not really that hungry afterward.

Regardless, you can see I still eat the same foods that I like to eat. I just added some healthy options in here and there. I did it slowly over time just like I'm asking you to do. This worked for me, and it can work for you too. Don't look at all these changes and get overwhelmed; that's what dissuades most people. It's like I said: These changes happened slowly over time.

If you look at the changes as a whole, they are big changes, but they weren't to me because of the pace of change I chose worked for me. It was something I was comfortable doing because I did it slow enough that I was ready for the change. I slowly phased out negative things and slowly added positive things.

I boiled the frog. That sucker is dead. I did it and you can too.

ME VS. THEE HILL

A journey of a thousand miles begins with a single step.

—Chinese Proverb

Is that really all it takes? Yes, it really is. As described previously, at the time I write this book I currently work as a project manager for a subsea search-and-salvage company that searches and recovers lost items or crashed aircraft called Phoenix International Holdings, Inc. They currently hold the contract for the US Navy SUPSALV and are hired usually multiple times a year to go and recover aircraft or items lost in the ocean.

This job, needless to say, takes me all over the world. I have only not been to two continents, and they most likely will remain unvisited by me, Antarctica, and Africa. I was born and raised in Lansing, Michigan. We grew up in winters that could reach -40 degrees Fahrenheit. Knowing and living in the perils of extreme cold, I can't think of a less appealing place to go than Antarctica (my toes and fingers are tingling just thinking about it).

Moreover, having met my wife in the Philippines (Manila) and being slapped in the face by the heat and humidity every time you step outside the comfort of the air conditioning, Africa is as equally not appealing. Not to mention other things that happen there frequently like beheadings, dismemberments, landmines, etc.

I'm sure there are nice places, but it's just not for me. I'm traveled out. I had, at one time, enough frequent flier miles to take myself and my wife from Manila, Philippines, to Honolulu, Hawaii (for one week), to Houston, Texas, to Baltimore, Maryland, absolutely free of charge. Moreover, from Philippines to Hawaii we rode first class (she was spoiled on her first airplane ride). The trip cost me 250,000 frequent flier miles in total and about $50 in cash.

The circumference of the entire Earth is 24,901 miles directly in the middle. At that time (and this was almost ten years ago now), I had enough frequent flier miles to circle the Earth at its widest point over ten times. Yeah, I fly a lot, and have continued flying since then, not as much, but regularly indeed.

Regardless of my travel proclivities, let's just say I'm cooped up on a plane, or in a line, or in a cab, or on a bus, or on a train, or living on a ship with nowhere to go. From 2019 to present (2021), there has been an ongoing operation in the Gulf of Mexico with our Autonomous Underwater Vehicle (AUV) contracting to another AUV company that lost their functionality of their own AUV, so they leased our Artemis AUV and a few of our personnel to oversee it.

In 2021 alone, due to periodic weather and sea states not conducive to safely conduct AUV operations, I have flown back and forth to New Orleans, Louisiana, sixteen times. I was stationed on the Echo Offshore vessel *Nikola* from December 26 until May 1, 2021 and then I finally said that was enough and I needed to be relieved. Having done roughly the same the year before, I was really getting cabin fever.

During one of these weather standbys, we stayed in port to just wait it out instead of just flying home. That left a lot of hours in the day to kill, and it usually involved watching movies or shows on the operations area TV. I'm sure feeling just as cooped up as the rest of us, the chief mate, Gilbert, asked his son James and James' friend and crew mate Cory if they wanted to go for a walk. I overheard and invited myself.

We had been on the ship so long, all us Phoenix guys felt like they were part of the crew now. A long walk sounded like a great idea with all this time to kill and having stayed on the same 128-foot vessel for months. Just a simple walk to the end of the pier and back was a little over a mile or so, I didn't really keep track.

There was some talking at first, but eventually, we just enjoyed the sounds of the gulf. The birds scavenging—or trying to, at least.

This particular day, it was really windy (part of the reason we were not operating at that time), and the birds were practically flying in place, and it was quite entertaining to watch them try to fly forward and end up turning around and flying at the speed of sound with the wind. It seemed like it anyway.

Other than the wind, it was a really nice day, and with the heat of southern Louisiana sun on our face and the fresh breeze cooling us down, we mostly just walked and enjoyed. It was during this walk that I decided I needed more of the open outdoors. I have felt entombed for most of my career stuck on ships, stuck on airplanes, stuck in airports, and the freedom and openness of the open road was completely appealing.

I can't remember exactly what day that was, but I know that when I came back, it was approximately May 1, and I was going to do this more often. Even when I was home between operations, I would coop myself up again inside my own house in my recliner. Enough coops. I was tired of cooping. I want that space, I want the sun on my face, I want the breeze at my back and at my front, I want that fresh air.

A couple of years back, one of my good friends, Jeremy (Hi! I'm Tom!), had purchased a Fitbit and would constantly go on about his ten thousand steps. I had no idea what he was talking about, but it seemed to make him happy so I would walk with him around the shop, and we would discuss things (at length and at random topics) when we were between operations and not busy.

I remembered that time, but I didn't go for the Fitbit right away. I had decided I was going to start to walk my ten thousand steps and get out into the world. I was using the Health App on my iPhone to track my steps at that time. As I said, I began just walking more around the shop and walking to the store for things we needed like bread or milk.

Just to give you an idea, ten thousand was almost double what I averaged before, so I knew it would have an effect. That was just how many steps I took previously without being conscious of them. Here is a chart from my Health App data. You can see that I ramped up my step count when I returned home in May, and you can see the spike from our walks on the pier in April.

Month (2021)	Average Steps Per Day
January	4231
February	4248
March	5604
April	6483
May	12327
June	19728
July	20565
August	13270
September (COVID quarantine)	8965
October	13141

You can see how my steps ramped up as I went farther and farther culminating to my farthest walk on record at one time: July 28, I walked 10.18 miles. It took me 2:57:14 at a 17'26" pace and accounted for 18,927 steps and burned 1,700 calories. I was completely over the moon. I was tired, but I did it. Ten miles in one walk had become my Everest and I scaled it.

While I was feeling very accomplished, I could only keep looking at that number. Three hours. Three hours out of my day to go for a walk. I had met my goal, but my increasing distance goals were taking up a lot of my time. When I returned, even my wife mentioned it.

"You were gone a long time this time," she said.

"I know," I said. "That was the longest I ever went, that was my distance goal and I met it."

It was then I decided, it's time to turn up the heat on this frog a little bit. That's how it should feel when you're ready to step things up to the next level, you should either accomplish a goal or just feel it is time. It's up to you. That's how I knew it was time to quicken the pace and start running some during my outings. It was then I changed my goals from steps to distance. I understood my walking had got me to the shape to be able to walk that distance in the blistering heat, I should be able to throw in some bouts of running along the way.

As I said, that was July 28, and you can see on the chart my steps took a downturn during August and that was because I started going for five miles at a time instead of ten. This was when I changed from ten thousand steps per day to doing ten thousand steps all at once, as I mentioned earlier. I also got my regular non-exercising steps throughout the day, but I started not counting them toward my daily step goals on days I ran. They were just "bonus steps."

Instead of just walking the ten thousand steps, I would run as far as I could periodically with my two-and-a-half-liter water pack on my back weighing about eight pounds completely full. (You can get about four and a half water bottles in that pack, which I drank almost all of during that record-setting ten-mile hike, but it was July and over 90 degrees, so that is a given).

I kept working at it all through August, increasing and increasing my running over walking. I had found a route that was 4.78 miles, it would only include two crossings of major roads (both with crosswalks), and it had four intense hills periodically throughout the route. It was perfect, and that's the route I still use today. Eventually, I changed it slightly, instead of turning left onto Maureen Lane, going to Madeley, going to Moylan, I just kept going down Millstream Drive past Maureen Lane and straight to Moylan Drive. (I know you don't know these roads, but I'm trying to be accurate, so you know this is really what I did. Besides you can look it up on Bowie maps and follow along, just don't come to my house, please; that's rude.) This slight change allowed me less turns, which is preferred when running, so could keep a good pace longer. This also went a little more direct and it ended up being about 4.83 miles total.

The hills I mentioned were always a challenge. If you have never been to Maryland, it has a lot of hills. Every time I run, I am credited with climbing about thirty-five to forty-five sets of stairs just by the Fitbit accounting for the rise in altitude (forty-seven total yesterday).

Thee Hill, going up route 450, just after the road that leads to Free State mall, was a challenge even when I was walking. This was the bottleneck in my ultimate plan to run the entirety of the 4.78–4.83-mile course.

There is something I didn't mention before, probably because it's embarrassing, and that is a power phrase. Whenever I am at the wall or at my limits during exercise, I have a power phrase I use to get me through it. It's my phrase; it works for me. I know I'm still not saying what it is. I say it one word at a time to really emphasis it. I understand I'm out in public, so I say it in my head. With the headphones blaring, I probably couldn't hear it out loud anyway, so I figured, I can just think it and it will be just as affective.

On one particular day, September 7, 2021, I was doing good. I was going at a good pace and just as I reached the crosswalk the light changed to the walking man "go" sign to cross. I steeled myself up for the climb of the long hill and dropped gears down and started up the hill. It's not a particularly steep hill, but it is long and arduous slow uphill climb. I had difficulty and was out of breath just walking up this hill. If I had to guess, it's about a quarter to a third of a mile long and the equivalent of climbing two to three sets of stairs.

I do have to point out, that at this point, I *had* gotten up this hill without stopping. What I hadn't done at that point, was to be able to continue running *after* this hill. It spent all my energy to the point my heartrate was peaked at 175 bpm, and I was just out of energy to keep running. Every time so far and I had to walk through the Hill Top Plaza (see what I mean about this hill? They even named the plaza after this hill) to the crosswalk on Race Track Road to catch my breath and give my heart a rest.

About halfway up the hill, I felt the wall coming again, but I was so close. I pushed through the pain and dropped down another gear, I reached back for what I had left in reserve and went for it. I did the opposite of what everything in my body wanted. It wanted to stop; I did the very opposite.

I keep my own "workouts" playlist, about fifty to sixty songs that are all upbeat or motivating songs, and I always shuffle them, so they come completely at random. As I reached for the next song switch on my headphones, which entails holding the volume up button for about three seconds, I literally said out loud, "Okay, random song gods, I need you." They delivered.

"Eye of the Tiger" by Survivor started in my ears. That distinct guitar opening that any fan of *Rocky III* will tell you is the epitome of motivating workout songs fired through my head. I said, "Hell yes," (only I didn't say "Hell") and accelerated. I was not getting up this hill; I was conquering it. This hill had become my bitch. As I was nearing the top of the hill, I used my power phrase, not to get me through it, but in ecstatic celebration. KING. KONG. AIN'T. GOT. NOTHING. ON. ME!

I powered over the top of the hill and kept running and even pounded my chest a couple of times and said "Yes!" I kept going, through Hill Top Plaza, to the crosswalk, the crosswalk was a walking man go (just like every other cross walk was the whole run, it was meant to be), across Race Track Road, up to the parking lot of the Cornerstone Church, back down through the parking lot, back to Race Track road, up *that* hill, up to Yorktown drive, turning on Yarmouth Lane, back to York Lane, up *that* hill, and back to my house panting, exhausted.

I did it. I beat the hill and kept going! I beat *all* the hills and I ran the whole way, 4.78 miles in 51:15 minutes at a 10'42" pace. It's hard to be exhausted. It's even harder to be exhausted and emotional. This was not the Olympics by any stretch of the imagination, but I am a *huge* fan of them. You watch as the people that have trained their whole lives for that one moment cross the line or make the shot or lift the weight, and they just have this release of achievement at the end of the culmination of all that hard work, and it just overcomes them with joy on top of their exhaustion. I felt exactly what I sensed those people felt having seen it a hundred times. I finally felt it and understood. I didn't have a medal to show for it, but I felt it hanging from my neck, nonetheless.

You are being pulled in two different directions between elation and exhaustion, but overall, I felt victorious. Besides, another great thing about being in shape is you recover very quickly. So after a few minutes of pacing in my backyard to cool down, I gathered myself and went inside for my protein shake, content with just sharing my achievement with my wife and daughter. That was my gold medal, that was my fulfillment, that was, at that time, as Vince Lombardi said, my finest hour.

> *I firmly believe that any man's finest hour, the greatest fulfillment of all that he holds dear, is that moment when he has worked his heart out in a good cause and lies exhausted on the field of battle—victorious.*
> —Vince Lombardi

CHANGING TACTICS TO CHALLENGE YOUR BRAIN

You have to slow boil the frog to keep it in the pot. However, you also have to change things up every now and then, or you will get bored and not have any fun, and when you don't have any fun, you'll want to find something else to do. Moreover, like I said, if you keep stepping up steps, it will take up a lot of your time.

I know there are some out there that say, "I'm just not a runner." Can you walk? Then you're a runner. Walking is just running at a slow pace. If you can walk, then you can jog which will lead to speeding up slowly over time, and all of a sudden, guess what? You are running. Stop looking at the end as a stage to dread. You are going to be ready by then. That is literally the point to slow boiling the frog. The things you're worried about on the tenth step above you will not seem that big a task if you're on the ninth step!

High Intensity Interval Training (HIIT) is something I just started, and I love it. It's not just running at my 9'30" to 10'30" jogging pace, it's getting on a treadmill and turning on some epic '90s rock like "I Won't Do That" by Meatloaf, and every time I really feel the music just hit the 9 or 10 speed button and sprint out those vibes!

It is really fun. It keeps the intensity level at a constant change, and it actually helps you increase your regular jogging pace. When you sprint, you run like you are supposed to run. Like you are running for your life from a predator, or you are running for your next meal and *that* thing is running for *its* life. Can you imagine if you had to do that every time you had to eat? Chase something running for its life? Sounds exhausting. But you see why fat animals in the wild are extremely rare; that's their plight on a daily basis. Look up Louis CK's bit about getting out of the food chain. It is hilarious, and there's some of that in this paragraph (language warning).

Regardless, those sprints awaken the muscles that have been dormant due to the fact that we don't have to run on a regular basis. I can do my five-mile run every day of the week and never feel the next-day muscle ache, but when I sprint, my glutes definitely feel it. That's another tip, if you want a nicer butt (nicer doesn't mean good, just nicer), you have to sprint (take a look at sprinters and take a look at the marathon runners, you'll see).

Jogging just works the smaller muscles in your butt, but when you "get up on a plane" running full speed and put the hammer down, the larger muscles in your glutes are driving you and they take the load of work. You may not be a runner, but if I tell you it will make your butt nicer, I bet you'll be sprinting tomorrow. But that's the point! When you are ready, you are ready. You can't skip to the end and get the rewards; you have to go on the whole journey to find out who you are and then get the rewards.

Point being, it's a constant evolutionary process. If you feel like you are in a rut and not making progress, then change it up! If you can't increase your pace anymore, then add weights to your arms or ankles. If you have maxed out your walking distance, then carry a ruck sack. My buddy John goes rucking all the time with fifty pounds on his back and swears by it. Everyone is different, and you literally have an endless supply of different things you can do to keep your interest up.

Go swimming, take up martial arts, go hiking, go rowing/use a row machine, use an elliptical, just name it! But keep your interest up to keep your motivation. Once you begin to see results, this will not be an issue.

One way I change it up that I do weekly is to change from body building or cardio during the work week, (Monday to Friday for most) and just do work around the house on Saturday and Sunday. Literally moving the earth. Earth moving exercises using a shovel and wheel barrow took up two-plus weekends of my time, and my body was exhausted, I actually took a rest day!

Exhausting the body is an unbelievable stress reducer. If you have a lot on your mind, find a project outside that you have been putting off because it is such a big job to do. I cleared out the garden that was there when we moved in to make room for a trampoline that my daughter really wanted. Even as big a project as that was, it led to other projects that were being held up because that one wasn't done. Now I have about two months' worth of weekend projects that I can do.

"*Chance favors only the prepared mind*" (Louis Pasteur). By this, he meant that sudden flashes of insight don't just happen but are the product of preparation. During all that work, even with your body exhausted, your mind is always troubleshooting. It has a stack of to do lists that it needs to sort out.

If you are doing menial tasks like shoveling and moving, sure, you'll be tired physically, but your mind is always trying to sort out your problems. We are usually so busy that we don't notice, so during these times when you are giving it your all in a slow meaningful effort, pay attention to where your mind keeps drifting to, and you may be rewarded with a solution to something you have been trying to solve. These slow yard tasks are just like walking a long straight-away during your walks, you will once again receive the benefits of problem solving while you work methodically. Away from distractions other than your work, your mind can be loud.

It's part of the reason that I ask for technology to be slowly cut out just like you are trying to cut out foods that are counterproductive. As great as it is to have that convenience, it is also one of the reasons we are all so stressed. Everything is right now, but you have to get out of that mindset. You have to be in the mindset that, yes, you have a problem, but it is not insurmountable. It is conquerable. These kinds of outdoor projects fit the bill exactly. You are focused on chipping away to finish but understand it doesn't have to all be done in one day or right now. Just keep working on it, just like everything else.

This goes back to getting your mind right (doesn't it always?), you have to take things one step at a time and become the most patient version of yourself. Challenging a stressed-out mind will work out the knots in there just like proper exercise and stretching will work out a muscle knot caused by stress. Just let things happen at their own pace, and when you start to do that, it will affect other parts of your life as well.

You'll stop stressing over small inconveniences like someone not paying attention at a stop light because they are one their phone. Instead of screaming at these people and laying on the horn, you give two little taps with your horn.

Wait, no one else here screamed at people while driving? Guess that was just me, I forgot not everyone is a hothead like I used to be (Okay, I still do it. PUT DOWN YOUR PHONES AND DRIVE PEOPLE! We literally stopped ten seconds ago!). My periodic road rage at technology aside, that's okay even if you still have some anger, it's healthy to let it out when it's justified.

Point being, part of that anger is what I discussed before about being unfulfilled, feeling unaccomplished. And people on their phones, sheesh, for real, ten seconds at a stop light and people whip out their phones. You can't wait a minute without being entertained, really? With this regiment of stepping it up and keeping things interesting, that daily accomplishment will be fulfilled, and you will be fulfilled.

I really do believe that this mentality and healthy lifestyle choice can solve so many basic problems that everyone seems to be suffering from. We still haven't really adjusted to being out of the food chain, especially with everything being so convenient now. We have way less challenges than we used to, and the brain is a designed problem solver. If it's not working on surviving, it's nitpicking on every other little detail in our lives, and it can be depressing analyzing every hole you have in your own life. So give it something to do!

When I'm driving, I always have some kind of audiobook playing. About everything and anything I want to learn about. Keeping your mind occupied with learning and challenges is like feeding chocolate cake to a screaming toddler. Your brain *needs* something to focus on, and if it doesn't have that, it starts focusing on where it lives—*you.* That's when the metaphorical tantrums start, and it begins overanalyzing its existence.

> You can't take life too seriously; you'll never make
> it out alive…write that down.
> —Van Wilder

Anyone who hasn't watched *Van Wilder* should do so. It's not only hilarious it really does have a lot of good quotes and philosophies you can pick and choose to adopt. I still use quotes from that movie; obviously, I just did. But don't worry!

> Worrying is like sitting in a rocking chair. It gives
> you something to do, but you don't really get
> anywhere…write that down.
> —Van Wilder

That is exactly what your brain is doing when it's worrying. It's trying to anticipate upcoming challenges because it is currently unchallenged. That's why you have to constantly change tactics because your brain will adapt to changes over time, so you have to mix it up. Same goes for your muscles, they pick up what you're putting down eventually and stop improving because you are giving them the exact same challenge to overcome. That's why I do so many different things when I work out during the week.

MY TYPICAL WORKOUT WEEK

I always start with stretching to get loose, no matter what I am doing. "Rule No. 18: Limber Up," from *Zombieland*. The stretching routine is exactly the same when I run and when I work out; only when I run, it stops at a certain point and I throw on my water sack and just take off (sometimes forgetting things to my detriment, like putting on sunblock or sweat band or extra towel to wipe off…whatever)

When I am working out for muscle building, I throw in some isometric back workouts and ab workouts while I'm down there on the mat. Isometrics is just holding your muscle under tension in a working position.

For example, lift up an arm. Easy, right? Okay, well, hold your arm up there for five minutes. Not so easy now, is it? Same principle in holding a pose while lying face down, lifting your arms and legs off of the mat. Your back will be on fire after thirty to sixty seconds. It's great for increasing lower back strength. I know, sounds boring, but I have my headphones on the whole time, and I'm usually singing. My neighbors can probably confirm.

Not only am I working out my singing chops, I'm making it fun and keeping my mind challenged in multiple ways. I'm keeping it occupied with a bevy of things that will keep my mind off of how much this *should* suck but it doesn't. I'm working out *and* having fun, but I digress. This is my current typical workout week. That's the easy way to lay it out because if I updated it every time I changed it, I would never get this book out there. So for now, I'll go through what I currently do.

Some of these I do supersets, which means if there are two sets of each exercise I will do one set of one exercise immediately followed by the set for the other exercise. For example, when I do bench presses, I immediately follow that with another exercise, then take a rest, and do both sets back-to-back again.

- Monday—Running
  - o Stretching and jumping jacks to warm up.
  - o Five-mile run on my normal course (5.22 miles now, thanks very much)
    - Even as I write this book, you can see how they scale up slowly. It was 4.77, then I said I upped it to 4.83. Now this update, I changed routes again to 5.22 miles.
- Tuesday—Muscle Building, Full Body Workout (This can change depending on time or injuries)
  - o Stretching, ab and back mat workouts.
  - o Full body stretching with resistance bands to strengthen and loosen small typically unused muscles.
  - o Curl-Ups and Pull-Ups until failure—two sets
    - Note: Pull-ups are my worst exercise. I use a bar that attaches to my door frame, stand on my tiptoes, and jump to help myself get over the bar. This works your calves as well. My aim is to train my muscles slowly until it gets used to moving the full load, otherwise, I would only do one pull-up. Using this method, I can do sets of eight, and it actually adds a cardio affect because you're using your whole body to get up there in the beginning, not just your back and shoulders.
  - o Resistance band core training (superset with curl-ups and pull-ups)
    - I step on my smaller resistance band with my heels so the band can go behind me, then I take both hands to lift the band above my head, and I lean backward. This is an isometric exercise,

you just hold this in place as long as you can and move the bands around to change the angle and work as many muscles as you possible can.

- I usually change positions with my hands making the positions wider or closer together to work different muscles. This is just a feel-out process and will differ per person.

o Dead Lift—six to eight reps (two sets)

- This usually requires a great deal of weight, but you can get the same results in the beginning by using resistance bands. In fact, I highly recommend using resistance bands in the beginning because this uses *a lot* muscles you don't normally use, and you need to get used to it.

  - You have to be very careful with this exercise, and it's uses almost your entire body except the chest. You will feel exactly what I mean.

- Using heavy dumbbells or a trap bar or resistance bands, you will squat down (*not bend down*), with your back straight, grab the weight, and stand straight up. Then return the weight almost back to the ground and repeat.

  - The reason I say be careful is because the idea of this exercise is to use as heavy a weight or as much resistance as you possibly can to get the maximum affect.

    o I have personally injured my back doing this exercise because I increased the weight to fast. I did not slow boil the frog and I was out of commission for a month. So, take this very slow.

o Trap Row—two sets (Super Set with Dead lift)

- Using dumbbells, lean forward (either sitting or standing) at a 45–60-degree angle and pull your arms straight up and out to maximize the effect on the traps and the mid back muscles.

- Think of a bench press how your arms should go outward and down instead of straight down, it's just going the completely opposite direction as a bench press. You are leaning forward and doing a reverse bench press basically.

o Incline Bench Press Setting No. 1—two sets, super slow until failure

- Using dumbbells, lean back against the bench with your head resting as well, slowly lower the weights down and to the side until even with or just below your chest. Slowly raise the weights back to the regular position.

  - I use very slow reps, and I can feel the stretching and working of the pectoral muscles. I don't even count; I just feel it. Once I get to the point where I struggle to get the weights back to the starting position, I do one more rep, but I use other muscles to help, like stomping on the floor or slightly doing a sit-up, whatever it takes to get that last rep. These are called *forced reps*. A technique used by the most symmetrical man to ever lift weights and multiple Mr. Universe title holder, Arnold Schwarzenegger. (No, I did not spell that right the first time. Sorry, Arnie.)

    o *Note: Everyone who has ever exercised and has been successful has a different way that they do bench presses and everything else for that matter. Everyone swears this is the way that works, and they are not lying. Because everyone is different. I tried doing it other people's way and didn't get any results, so I tried different things until I found what works for me. Same will go for you, but what works for me is what and how I described. There is an endless supply of ways to do things. Just look up how-to videos, and you will see there's a dozen different ways to do every exercise.*

o Incline Curls—two sets (superset with incline bench press)
   ▪ Using the same incline setting on the bench and lighter weights, lean back with your arms at your side and curl the weight upward and flex the bicep.
      • The incline will not only stretch your arms to avoid the permanent angle on your arms, but it will add to the work load on the bicep.
         o If you work your biceps and don't stretch them out, your arms will start to bend inward all of the time. You can see this in some body builders.
o Incline Bench Press Setting No. 2—two sets, super slow until failure
   ▪ Exact same as Setting No. 1, but at less of an incline. Lower the incline one setting more toward the ground. This will be the same all the way down until a regular bench press position laying completely flat.
   ▪ Use the same slow reps as the first setting and use forced reps to get one to two more reps than just using proper form.
o Resistance Band Stretching (Super set with Setting No. 2)
   ▪ Using a resistance band (same as the isometric core training), stretch the band over your head then rotate it until it is directly behind you.

Going to sound strange but start flapping your arms straight forward and straight back to give your pecs a stretch and your mid back some work load as well.

- Play with the angles as well to fully stretch and engage from all angles. Please see pictures if this is unclear.

o Incline Bench Press Setting No. 3—two sets, super slow until failure

- Exact same as Setting No. 2, but at less of an incline. Lower the incline one setting more toward the ground.

- Use the same slow reps as the first setting and use forced reps to get one to two more reps than just using proper form.

o Lat pull-down—two sets, eight to ten reps (Superset with Setting No. 3)

- I use resistance bands hooked up to my pull up bar at home for this, but if at a gym, there are always lat pull-down machines.

- Sit or kneel beneath your pull-up bar/lat pull-down machine and grab the handles. Lean back at a 30- to 45-degree angle and pull it toward your chest.

- Slowly pull toward yourself and hold at the maximum for a count, squeezing your shoulder blades together, and return to start.

o Bench Press Fully Flat—two sets, super slow until failure.

- Same as the first three setting only you are completely flat now.

- Use the same slow reps as the first setting and use forced reps to get one to two more reps than just using proper form.

o Shoulder Gauntlet—two sets, five to eight reps per stage (Superset with Bench press)

- *"Spartans! Prepare for glory!"*—King Leonidas, from the movie *300.*
- This not only supersets with the bench press, it's a super duper set all on its own and will test every facial muscle you have. Use light weights to start this—I mean like 2.5 to 5 pounds, and you will feel why. I use ten-pound weights for this but have been doing it a long time, and it still hurts.
- Every stage listed will be done immediately following the previous stage, no stopping, no rest. That is why I call this the Shoulder Gauntlet.
- Start with your arms at your sides and lift each arm to shoulder level and bring back down to your side five to eight reps, keeping your arms as straight as possible (choose your rep total and make it the same for each following stage, I use eight reps).
- Immediately switch by putting your arms in front of your hips and lifting straight up over each shoulder, your arms can be at a small angle for more support. Same reps as first stage.
- Immediately bend to a 75 to 90 degree and pull the weights outward and back toward your shoulder blades keeping your arms as straight as possible. Same reps as other stages.
- Immediately stand up straight up with your arms at your side and lift straight up in front of keeping your arms as straight as possible and lift until level with the shoulders. Same reps as other stages.
- Immediately get on your tip toes and bend your waist at a 45-degree angle and use angled arms to pull the weights toward your shoulder blades. Same reps as other stages.

- Immediately stand straight up and lift the weights up to your sides with your palms facing up and your elbows at a 90-degree angle at shoulder level and press straight up.
- Your shoulders should be on fire right now. If they are not, use more weight next time.
  - Goblet Squat—two sets, slow reps eight to ten
    - Using a dumbbell that you can hold in front of you, grab the dumbbell with both hands and put it out directly in front of you as far as you can and maintain that position throughout the set.
    - Keeping the weight straight out, squat down as far as you can and as slowly as you can and return. Repeat this for eight to ten reps.
  - Curl and Press—two sets, regular reps eight to ten.
    - Begin with the weights at your sides and curl each arm at the same time until you flex the bicep.
    - Immediately turn your wrists and press the weight straight up over your head. Return the weight safely back to your side and repeat eight to ten reps.
  - Farmer's Carry—two reps, distance or failure
    - If you don't have a lot of space, you can simply walk in place, but you need to walk to do this.
    - Get some heavy weights or as heavy as you can and carry them around while walking for a set distance or set amount of time, you choose which you like. I walk around my workout room until my hands are screaming at me to let go.
      - You will feel that this works about as much if not more as the dead lift, tweak your weight load and your distance to get the full effect of this exercise.
  - Thrusters—two sets, eight to ten explosive reps
    - Get a weight you know you can press without help and go one size higher. If you can do shoul-

der presses with thirty-pound weights then use thirty-five-pound weights for this.

- Start with the weights at shoulder level with palms up and elbows at a 90-degree angle.
- Squat down as far as you can and then explode upward. In one continuous motion, use the momentum of the squat to thrust the weights over your head as high as you can and let that momentum lift up onto your toes.
- You are looking to apply almost enough force to make yourself jump but hold just enough back to keep your toes on the ground.
- This exercise will work almost everything, and you will probably be gasping for air by the end of the set. It definitely adds a cardio effect to the end.

o Bicep gauntlet—one super set until failure

- This will be much easier to do in an actual gym, but you can do the same if you have enough weights at home.
- The gauntlet involves running the rack from heaviest to lightest curling as many times as you can. I always start the reps with my left arm because it will fail first due to permanent nerve damage I have on that side that makes it always just a little bit weaker than my right arm.
- Start with the heaviest weight you can curl standing up and curl it until you can't curl it anymore without losing form, changing arms each rep.
- Put that weight down and grab the next one in line and curl that until failure alternating each arm per rep.
- Continue doing this until you either reach the lowest weight on the rack or you just can't curl anymore.
- This is a finishing set, always do this last because you will be completely spent after this.

- Wednesday—Running
  o Stretching and jumping jacks to warm up.
  o Five-mile run on my normal course
- Thursday—Muscle Building, Full Body Workout
  - All the same as the first time
- Friday—Running: HIIT training.
- Saturday—Yard work/House Work
- Sunday—Yard work/House Work/ or rest

The following week, I will swap the schedule during the "work week" days, so I run Tuesday and Thursday and do my workouts three times a week, and sometimes during those weeks, I will throw in HIIT on Friday anyway cause it's new and fun right now!

I can already hear the tumblers of your brains turning and grinding: "I'm not doing all of that!" Well, neither did I when I started, and this is just a full list of what I usually do. Granted as stated above, sometimes I have time constraints or just don't feel 100 percent, so I don't always do all of it, but more than once, I have cranked all of that out in one day. The rest of the time, I mix and match which to do especially on days I do the full body workout three times a week.

I didn't work out with weights until I met my weight loss goal, then I started changing from just weight loss to muscle building and 10 percent body fat. It grew over time, and the workouts I listed actually takes about as much time as my run does, just over an hour.

Sure, it runs over sometimes when I get into free form post workout resistance band training, which is just keeping tension on a band as I move it in every direction possible trying to separate every part of me from every other part of me. Just something I do if I'm not completely spent, and it gives a great post workout cool down and stretch out. It's especially appealing to just do whatever after such a strict regimen to follow.

What did I say earlier in the chapter? Don't look at the tenth step from the first step and say it's too high. It *is* too high when you first start, but that's not the next step. Your current step/goal is the only thing you should be focused on with one eye on the next step when you are ready to go up.

This is just my example so you can see what I am doing now. By the time you are reading this, it will probably be different because of the constant changes. Some of these are considered advanced tactics that you elevate to eventually, not where you start. You shouldn't even lift a single dumbbell until you have reached your target weight. Even then, you don't have to! Just maintain your regimen to keep your weight. These workouts are advanced so I can take my body to the next level because I want to go there.

You never have to go anywhere you don't want to go and that includes weight training. You can reach your weight goals just by low- to medium-impact activities like walking, jogging, rowing, or swimming. Find your niche that you can accomplish your goals. These are just examples of things I do to give ideas to those who *do* want to go to the next level.

With the exception to when I say to use heavy weights, all of my weight training is with lower weights because I use so many reps throughout the entire workout, and so I can use proper form and move very slowly to maximize the muscle effort. I only use about forty-pound weights (right now) for all my bench presses (each arm), I just perform them super slow to maximize the effect of the exercise. I may change it up someday, but that's what I do right now.

That's all you ever can do, do your best today while keeping one eye out for tomorrow.

IF YOU HAVEN'T ACTED YET, IT'S TIME

I have shown you exactly what I have done from the beginning until now, hopefully. You have a general road map that you can take the same journey. Take what I said to you and evolve it into something that will work for you. Most others will have a much more difficult time than I did starting out, but it doesn't matter. As long as you are taking strides in the right direction, you will get there.

I'm not an expert, at all. I used the tools and knowledge anyone else can. I'm just an average guy that figured out a long-term method to meet every goal you set as long as you just keep moving forward with your plans, no matter how long they take. I didn't sign up for a super-secret weight-loss program, and I didn't take weight-loss pills to achieve this. I just found a way to start a routine and slowly change and evolve it to make it more effective and keep moving my body in the direction it needed to.

I like to go through a whole book at a time, even when it's asking me to do things along the way. I believe I have written this book in a manner that would allow people like me to do that. So that's why this section is titled that way. You now have all the information you need to succeed. Knowledge without action is wasted opportunity.

Are you going to take this knowledge and use it or are you going to find an excuse not to do so? I hope not. I use this phrase to myself to keep me motivated to keep moving forward: "What would the *old* me do in this situation?" The old me would take this knowledge and try and find a way to dismiss it. Try to find a way to convince myself that this would not work for me because of this or because of that. The old me would not even try.

Don't be the person you are trying to leave behind, that person wants you to destroy yourself and should not be listened to in any instance. That person wants you to quit. That person wants you to fail. Winners have results and losers have excuses. The very reason I start this book with the Dylan Thomas poem is to remind you to not go quietly into the night, but to shine in the daylight. To look toward the brighter side of things, to stop slowly killing yourself. Save your own life, things don't have to be bleak—that's your choice.

If you read this whole book and still find excuses, then I'm sorry, you're a loser. If you want to spit in my face right now because I called you a loser, then I've done my job, and I'm not worried about you. I'm worried about *you*. Yes, *you*. The one who is still making excuses, the one who is still skeptical and on the fence sitting on their fat ass, probably eating some potato chips *right now*. Anyone can do this, anyone. Even Potato Chip Fingers over there. Yeah, wipe it on your shirt too. Jeez, what a slob.

Today's effort is tomorrow's body. Period. Minimal effort will result in minimal results.

Maximum effort!
—Deadpool

Just like when you ask a rich person if money can buy happiness, they will say, "Well, I've been rich and I've been poor, and I will take rich every time." Well, I have been over weight and I have been in shape, and I will take in shape every time.

A winner will take this info and change their life for the better and permanently. A loser will find any and all excuses why it worked for me and others, but it won't work for them.

So which is it? Are you a winner or are you a loser?

EPILOGUE

Boil the Frog was a literal joy to write. I really can't wait for people to start giving me feedback on how they are doing and how much they have accomplished because they read this book. Special thanks to all the people I mentioned in this book, especially my *best* (happy, Craig?) friends, Craig Turner and Jeremy Blake, who let me bounce ideas off of them. You know you have true friends when they can tell you something that you would punch a stranger for saying but are really grateful that your friend said it because they truly have your best interest at heart.

Also special thanks to my wife, Jenny, and daughter, Brianna, that completely supported me on this journey and continue to do so. As I said, this will completely change your life, so this is just what I do now and they understand that. It's part of our lives that I disappear for an hour or two each day to work on myself to keep that monster I used to be away.

This book and the strategies inside can be used in any instance. I hope some people out there can use these methods to fight addiction, like I did. I still drink, but now I drink to enjoy it, not to get drunk. Use these tactics however you can help your lives. It can work for you, just like Novocain, it always works if you just give it enough time just like Denzel Washington says in *Remember the Titans*. Paraphrased of course.

Speaking of Denzel, another great thing to remember is this: "*You will never be criticized by someone who is doing more than you. You'll always be criticized by someone doing less. Remember that*" (Denzel Washington).

I am going to start a vlog to start documenting my journey after this book is fully completed and ready to print. It will be called "Boil the Frog," obviously. I will also set up a Facebook page (also Boil the Frog) for you all to join and post and share your progress, because as harsh as I can be, it's tough love. I really do, from the bottom of my heart, want to help you get to where you want to go.

Until you reach your goals, I'm not your friend, I am temporarily your coach. While you are training, I will be your cheerleader, and when you finally Boil the Frog cross that finish line, I hope to be your hero.

So go forth, my friends. Be safe, be committed, and be disciplined. Just don't forget that the struggles we put ourselves through are to live life and enjoy things.

> *All work and no play makes Jack a dull boy.*
> —Stephen King, *The Shining*

I know you can do it, I believe in you, and I am already proud to be even a small part of your lives.

Dennis McVicker
November 17, 2021

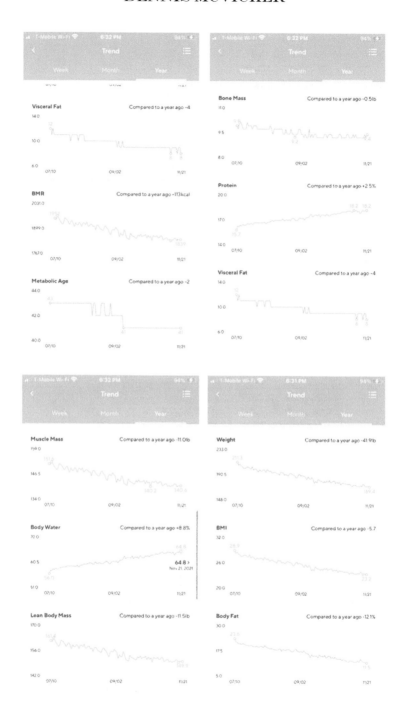

ABOUT THE AUTHOR

Dennis McVicker was born in Lansing, Michigan in 1977 on August 3. He graduated from J. W. Sexton High School in 1995. Bouncing from job to job, he found himself in a sad state of affairs for the next six years and ultimately decided to join the United States Navy in 2001 shortly before the 9/11 attacks on the World Trade Center.

Serving honorably for six years as a Petty Officer 2nd Class Fire Controlman, he left the Navy to join Phoenix International as an electronics technician on a Remotely Operated Vehicle (ROV) Deep Drone. This job took him all over the world, and he participated in over a dozen aircraft recoveries from helicopters to planes and from black boxes to tail rotors. Moreover, it allowed him to assist in bringing closure to family's victims by recovering the remains of the personnel on board.

This multitude of world traveling allowed him to accumulate a lot of frequent flier miles which he used to meet, court, and marry his wife, Jenny, from Manila, Philippines, after they met in an online chat room. Jenny and Dennis have a daughter together named Brianna, born in 2013.

He currently lives in Bowie, Maryland, and in 2020, he started Dawn Upon, an online business which changed his life. This newfound purpose working for himself led him to turn his life around and begin again. This led him to write his experiences down in hopes to help others find the same purpose that changed his life.

Printed in the USA
CPSIA information can be obtained
at www.ICGtesting.com
LVHW072353230324
775355LV00018B/388